grilled
and chilled

grilled
and chilled

120 delectable recipes for light and fresh summer cooking – lunches and suppers, picnics, barbecues, outdoor parties, al fresco dining and open-air entertaining

martha day

southwater

This edition is published by Southwater

Southwater is an imprint of Anness Publishing Ltd
Hermes House, 88–89 Blackfriars Road, London SE1 8HA
tel. 020 7401 2077; fax 020 7633 9499
www.southwaterbooks.com; info@anness.com

© Anness Publishing Ltd 1996, 2005

UK agent: The Manning Partnership Ltd, 6 The Old Dairy, Melcombe Road, Bath BA2 3LR;
tel. 01225 478444; fax 01225 478440; sales@manning-partnership.co.uk

UK distributor: Grantham Book Services Ltd, Isaac Newton Way, Alma Park Industrial Estate,
Grantham, Lincs NG31 9SD; tel. 01476 541080; fax 01476 541061; orders@gbs.tbs-ltd.co.uk

North American agent/distributor: National Book Network, 4501 Forbes Boulevard,
Suite 200, Lanham, MD 20706; tel. 301 459 3366; fax 301 429 5746; www.nbnbooks.com

Australian agent/distributor: Pan Macmillan Australia, Level 18, St Martins Tower,
31 Market St, Sydney, NSW 2000; tel. 1300 135 113; fax 1300 135 103;
customer.service@macmillan.com.au

New Zealand agent/distributor: David Bateman Ltd, 30 Tarndale Grove,
Off Bush Road, Albany, Auckland; tel. (09) 415 7664; fax (09) 415 8892

A CIP catalogue record for this book is available from the British Library.

Contributing authors: Catherine Atkinson, Maxine Clarke, Christine France,
Shirley Gill, Carole Handslip, Sue Maggs, Annie Nichols,
Jenny Stacey, Liz Trigg and Steven Wheeler

Publisher: Joanna Lorenz
Senior Cookery Editor: Linda Fraser
Assistant Editor: Emma Brown
Designer: Siân Keogh
Photographers: Karl Adamson, Edward Allright, James Duncan,
Michelle Garrett and Don Last
Stylists: Madeleine Brehaut, Hilary Guy and Fiona Tillett

For all recipes, quantities are given in both metric and imperial
measures, and, where appropriate, measures are also given in standard
cups and spoons. Follow one set, but not a mixture, because they are
not interchangeable.

Front cover shows grilled fennel - for method, see page 88.

Previously published as The All-Summer Cookbook

1 3 5 7 9 10 8 6 4 2

CONTENTS

INTRODUCTION

Summer is a wonderful season for the cook. At no other time of year is a more diverse and appealing assortment of fresh, natural produce available. From the freshest hand-picked berries and seasonal fruit to delicious sun-ripened vegetables and pungent garden herbs, all can be used to create a wonderful variety of sumptuous summer fare.

Whatever the occasion, from picnics to summer lunches, barbecues to garden parties, this inspiring collection is sure to provide the perfect dish. The chapters include delicious soups and light meals, spectacular salads, barbecue and picnic recipes, all sorts of pasta dishes, breads and pizzas, and, of course, summer desserts. In addition to classics such as Smoked Salmon Pâté, Salade Niçoise, Tandoori Chicken and Margherita Pizza, there are also exciting innovative recipes featuring some favourite ingredients: try Red Pepper and Watercress Filo Parcels, Warm Duck Salad with Orange and Coriander, and Salmon with Spicy Pesto. If you enjoy looking far afield for inspiration, you will find plenty here to please. There are lots of recipes from around the world, for example, Grilled Chicken with Pica de Gallo Salsa, Vietnamese Stuffed Squid, and Indonesian Pork and Peanut Satay.

All the recipes use high-quality, fresh produce and, from the simplest soup to the most contemporary salad, reflect and encapsulate the essence of summer. With so many wonderful ingredients to choose from, this tempting collection of recipes is sure to inspire, and the simple-to-follow, step-by-step format means that creating enticing summer meals becomes easy and enjoyable.

Pasta Shells with Tomatoes and Rocket

This attractive pasta dish relies for its success on the bright colour and peppery flavour of rocket, and the sweetest, ripest cherry tomatoes.

Serves 4

INGREDIENTS
450g/1 lb/4 cups pasta shells
450g/1lb ripe cherry tomatoes
75g/3oz fresh rocket (arugula)
45ml/3 tbsp olive oil
salt and ground black pepper
Parmesan cheese, to serve

olive oil

pasta shells

cherry tomatoes

Parmesan cheese

rocket

1 Cook the pasta in plenty of boiling salted water according to the manufacturer's instructions. Drain well.

2 Halve the tomatoes. Trim, wash and dry the rocket.

3 Heat the oil in a large pan, add the tomatoes and cook for barely 1 minute. The tomatoes should only just heat through and not disintegrate.

4 Shave the Parmesan cheese using a rotary vegetable peeler.

5 Add the pasta, then the rocket. Carefully stir to mix and heat through. Season well with salt and ground black pepper. Serve immediately with plenty of shaved Parmesan cheese.

Red Pepper and Watercress Filo Parcels

Peppery watercress combines well with sweet red pepper in these crisp little parcels.

Makes 8

INGREDIENTS
3 red (bell) peppers
175g/6oz watercress
225g/8oz/1 cup ricotta cheese
50g/2oz/¼ cup blanched almonds, toasted and chopped
8 sheets filo pastry
30ml/2 tbsp olive oil
salt and ground black pepper

ricotta

red pepper

watercress

almonds

filo pastry

1 Preheat the oven to 190°C/375°F/ Gas 5. Place the peppers under a hot grill (broiler) until charred. Place in a plastic bag. When cool enough to handle peel, seed and pat dry on kitchen paper.

2 Place the peppers and watercress in a food processor and pulse until coarsely chopped. Spoon into a bowl.

3 Mix in the ricotta and almonds, and season to taste.

4 Working with 1 sheet of filo pastry at a time, cut out 2 × 18cm/7in and 2 × 5cm/2in squares from each sheet. Brush 1 large square with a little olive oil and place a second large square at an angle of 90 degrees to form a star shape.

5 Place 1 of the small squares in the centre of the star shape, brush lightly with oil and top with a second small square.

6 Top with ⅛ of the red pepper mixture. Bring the edges together to form a purse shape and twist to seal. Place on a lightly greased baking sheet and cook for 25–30 minutes until golden.

Tagliatelle with Pea Sauce, Asparagus and Broad Beans

A creamy pea sauce makes a wonderful combination with the crunchy young vegetables.

Serves 4

INGREDIENTS
15ml/1 tbsp olive oil
1 garlic clove, crushed
6 spring onions (scallions), sliced
225g/8oz/1 cup frozen peas, thawed
350g/12oz fresh young asparagus
30ml/2 tbsp chopped fresh sage, plus extra leaves, to garnish
finely grated rind of 2 lemons
450ml/¾ pint/1¾ cups vegetable stock or water
225g/8oz frozen broad (fava) beans, thawed
450g/1lb tagliatelle
60ml/4 tbsp low-fat yogurt

1 Heat the oil in a pan. Add the garlic and spring onions and cook gently for 2–3 minutes until softened.

2 Add the peas and ⅓ of the asparagus, together with the sage, lemon rind and stock or water. Bring to the boil, reduce the heat and simmer for 10 minutes, until tender. Purée in a blender until smooth.

3 Meanwhile, remove the outer skins from the broad beans and discard.

lemon

garlic

asparagus

broad beans

peas

yogurt

tagliatelle

sage

spring onion

4 Cut the remaining asparagus into 5cm/2in lengths, trimming off any tough fibrous stems, and blanch in boiling water for 2 minutes.

5 Cook the tagliatelle following the instructions on the side of the packet until *al dente*. Drain well.

COOK'S TIP

Frozen peas and beans have been used here to cut down the preparation time, but the dish tastes even better if you use fresh young vegetables when in season.

6 Add the cooked asparagus and shelled beans to the sauce and reheat. Stir in the yogurt and toss into the tagliatelle. Garnish with a few extra sage leaves and serve.

Polenta and Baked Tomatoes

A staple of northern Italy, polenta is a nourishing, filling food, served here with a delicious fresh tomato and olive topping.

Serves 4–6

INGREDIENTS
2 litres/3½ pints/9 cups water
500g/1¼lb quick-cook polenta
12 large ripe plum tomatoes, sliced
4 garlic cloves, thinly sliced
30ml/2 tbsp chopped fresh oregano
    or marjoram
115g/4oz/½ cup black olives, pitted
30ml/2 tbsp olive oil
salt and ground black pepper

black olives

marjoram

plum tomatoes

garlic

oregano

polenta

1 Place the water in a large pan and bring to the boil. Whisk in the polenta and simmer for 5 minutes.

2 Remove the pan from the heat and pour the polenta into a 23 × 33cm/9 × 13in Swiss roll tin (jelly roll pan). Smooth out the surface with a metal spatula until level, and leave to cool.

3 Preheat the oven to 180°C/350°F/ Gas 4. With a 7.5cm/3in round pastry cutter, stamp out 12 rounds of polenta. Lay them so that they slightly overlap in a lightly oiled ovenproof dish.

4 Layer the tomatoes, garlic, oregano or marjoram and olives on top of the polenta, seasoning the layers as you go. Sprinkle with the olive oil, and bake uncovered for 30–35 minutes. Serve immediately.

Smoked Salmon Pâté

Making this pâté in individual ramekins wrapped in extra smoked salmon gives an extra special presentation. Taste the mousse as you are making it as some people prefer more lemon juice and seasoning.

Serves 4

INGREDIENTS
350g/12oz thinly sliced smoked
    salmon
150ml/¼ pint/⅔ cup double
    (heavy) cream
finely grated rind and juice of 1 lemon
salt and ground black pepper
Melba toast, to serve

lemon

smoked salmon

black pepper

salt

1 Line four small ramekin dishes with clear film (plastic wrap). Line with 115g/4oz of the smoked salmon, cut into strips long enough to flop over the edges.

2 In a food processor fitted with a metal blade, process the rest of the smoked salmon with the double cream, lemon rind and juice, and seasoning.

3 Pack the lined ramekins with the smoked salmon pâté and wrap over the loose strips of salmon. Cover and chill for 30 minutes, then turn out of the moulds and serve with Melba toast.

COOK'S TIP

Process the salmon in short bursts until it is just smooth. Don't over-process the paté or it will thicken too much.

Baked Herb Crêpes

These mouth-watering, light herb crêpes make a striking starter at a dinner party, but are equally splendid served with a crisp salad for lunch.

Serves 4

INGREDIENTS
25g/1oz chopped fresh herbs
   (such as parsley, thyme
   and chervil)
15ml/1 tbsp sunflower oil, plus extra
   for frying
100ml/4fl oz/½ cup skimmed milk
3 small (US medium) eggs
25g/1oz/¼ cup plain (all-purpose)
   flour
salt and ground black pepper

FOR THE SAUCE
30ml/2 tbsp olive oil
1 small onion, chopped
2 garlic cloves, crushed
15ml/1 tbsp grated fresh ginger root
400g/14oz can chopped tomatoes

FOR THE FILLING
450g/1lb fresh spinach
175g/6oz/¾ cup ricotta cheese
25g/1oz/2 tbsp pine nuts, toasted
5 halves sun-dried tomatoes in olive
   oil, drained and chopped
30ml/2 tbsp shredded fresh basil
nutmeg
4 egg whites

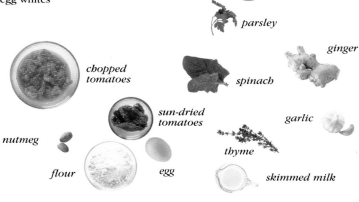

onion

parsley

chopped tomatoes

ginger

spinach

sun-dried tomatoes

nutmeg

garlic

thyme

flour

egg

skimmed milk

2 Heat a small non-stick crêpe or frying pan and add a very small amount of oil. Pour out any excess oil and pour in a ladleful of the batter. Swirl around to cover the base. Cook for 1–2 minutes, turn over and cook the other side. Repeat to make 8 crêpes.

3 To make the sauce, heat the oil in a small pan. Add the onion, garlic and ginger and cook gently for 5 minutes until softened. Add the tomatoes and cook for a further 10–15 minutes until the mixture thickens. Purée, strain and set aside.

1 To make the crêpes, place the herbs and oil in a blender and blend until smooth, pushing down any whole pieces with a spatula. Add the milk, eggs, flour and a pinch of salt and process again until smooth and pale green. Leave to rest for 30 minutes.

4 To make the filling, wash the spinach, removing any large stalks, and place in a large pan with only the water that clings to the leaves. Cover and cook, stirring once, until the spinach has just wilted. Remove from the heat and refresh in cold water. Place in a sieve (strainer) or colander; squeeze out the excess water and chop finely. Mix the spinach with the ricotta, pine nuts, sun-dried tomatoes and basil. Season with salt, nutmeg and ground black pepper.

5 Preheat the oven to 190°C/375°F/ Gas 5. Whisk the egg whites until stiff but not dry. Fold one-third into the spinach and ricotta to lighten the mixture, then gently fold in the rest.

6 Taking each crêpe at a time, place on a lightly oiled baking sheet. Place a large spoonful of filling on each one and fold into quarters. Repeat until all the filling and crêpes are used up. Bake in the oven for 10–15 minutes or until set. Reheat the tomato sauce to serve with the crêpes.

COOK'S TIP

If you prefer, use plain sun-dried tomatoes without any oil, and soak them in warm water for 20 minutes before using.

Ceviche

This is a fruity appetizer of marinated fresh fish. Take very special care in choosing the fish for this dish; it must be as fresh as possible and served on the same day it is made.

Serves 6

INGREDIENTS
350g/12oz cooked medium prawns
  (shrimp)
350g/12oz scallops, removed from
  their shells, with corals intact
350g/12oz salmon fillet
175g/6oz tomatoes
1 mango, about 175g/6oz
1 red onion, finely chopped
1 fresh red chilli
juice of 8 limes
30ml/2 tbsp caster (superfine)
  sugar
2 pink grapefruits
3 oranges
4 limes
salt and ground black pepper

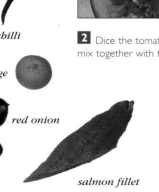

tomato *mango*

prawns

red chilli

scallops

orange

red onion

pink grapefruit *lime* *salmon fillet*

1 Peel the prawns and cut the scallops into 1.2cm/½in dice.

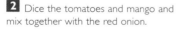

2 Dice the tomatoes and mango and mix together with the red onion.

3 Cut the fish into small pieces, dice the chilli and mix with the fish, tomato and mango. Add the lime juice, sugar and seasoning. Stir and leave to marinate for 3 hours.

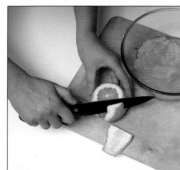

4 Segment the grapefruit, oranges and limes. Drain off as much excess lime juice as possible and mix the fruit segments into the marinated ingredients. Season to taste and serve.

Clam Chowder

Canned or bottled clams in brine, once drained, can be used as an alternative to fresh ones in their shells. During cooking, if any of the clam shells remain closed, discard them as they would have been dead before cooking.

Serves 4

INGREDIENTS
300ml/½ pint/1¼ cups double (heavy) cream
75g/3oz/6 tbsp unsalted (sweet) butter
1 small onion, finely chopped
1 apple, sliced
1 garlic clove, crushed
45ml/3 tbsp mild curry powder
350g/12oz baby corn
600ml/1 pint/2½ cups fish stock
225g/8oz new potatoes, peeled and cooked
24 baby (pearl) onions, peeled and boiled
40 small clams
salt and ground black pepper
8 lime wedges, to garnish

baby onion

potatoes

lime

curry powder

clams

apple

baby corn

1 Pour the cream into a small pan and cook over a high heat until it is reduced by half.

2 In a larger pan, melt half the butter. Add the onion, apple, garlic clove and curry powder. Sauté until the onion is translucent. Add the reduced cream and stir well.

3 In another pan, melt the remaining butter and add the baby corn. Cook for 5 minutes. Increase the heat and add the cream mixture, stock and cooked potatoes. Bring to the boil.

4 Add the baby onions and clams. Cover and cook until the clams have opened. Discard any that do not open. Season well to taste, and serve garnished with lime wedges.

Salade Niçoise

Salade Niçoise is a happy marriage of tuna, hard-boiled eggs, green beans and potatoes. Anchovies, olives and capers are often also included, but it is the first four ingredients that combine to make this a classic salad.

Serves 4

INGREDIENTS
700g/1½lb potatoes, peeled
225g/8oz green beans, trimmed
3 eggs, hard-boiled
1 cos or romaine lettuce
125ml/4fl oz French Dressing
225g/8oz small plum tomatoes, quartered
400g/14oz canned tuna steak in oil, drained
25g/1oz canned anchovy fillets
30ml/2 tbsp capers
12 black olives
salt and ground black pepper

1 Bring the potatoes to the boil in salted water and cook for 20 minutes. Boil the green beans for 6 minutes. Drain and cool the potatoes and beans under running water.

cos lettuce

green beans

olives

potatoes

anchovy fillets

plum tomatoes

capers

2 Slice the potatoes thickly. Shell and quarter the eggs.

3 Wash the lettuce and spin dry, then chop the leaves roughly. Moisten with half of the dressing in a large salad bowl.

4 Moisten the potatoes, green beans and tomatoes with dressing, then arrange them on top of the salad leaves.

COOK'S TIP

The ingredients for Salade Niçoise can be prepared well in advance, but should be assembled just before serving to retain flavour and freshness.

5 Break the tuna up with a fork and distribute over the salad with the eggs, anchovy fillets, capers and olives. Season to taste and serve.

Melon and Basil Soup

A deliciously refreshing chilled fruit soup, just right for a hot summer's day.

Serves 4–6

INGREDIENTS
2 Charentais or rock melons
75g/3oz/⅓ cup caster (superfine)
   sugar
175ml/6fl oz/¾ cup water
finely grated rind and juice of 1 lime
45ml/3 tbsp shredded fresh basil
fresh basil leaves, to garnish

basil

caster sugar

lime

Charentais melon

1 Cut the melons in half across the middle. Scrape out the seeds and discard. Using a melon baller, scoop out 20–24 balls and set aside for the garnish. Scoop out the remaining flesh and place in a blender or food processor.

2 Place the sugar, water and lime zest in a small pan over a low heat. Stir until dissolved, bring to the boil and simmer for 2–3 minutes. Remove from the heat and leave to cool slightly. Pour half the mixture into the blender or food processor with the melon flesh. Blend until smooth, adding the remaining syrup and lime juice to taste.

COOK'S TIP
Add the syrup in two stages, as the amount of sugar needed will depend on the sweetness of the melon.

3 Pour the mixture into a bowl, stir in the basil and chill. Serve garnished with basil leaves and melon balls.

Chilled Fresh Tomato Soup

This effortless uncooked soup can be made in minutes.

Serves 4–6

INGREDIENTS

1.5kg/3–3½lb ripe tomatoes, peeled
   and roughly chopped
4 garlic cloves, crushed
30ml/2 tbsp extra virgin olive oil
   (optional)
30ml/2 tbsp balsamic vinegar
4 slices wholemeal (whole-wheat)
   bread
low-fat yogurt, to garnish
ground black pepper

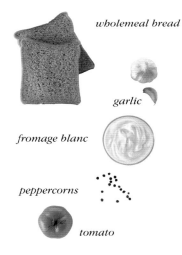

wholemeal bread

garlic

fromage blanc

peppercorns

tomato

COOK'S TIP

For the best flavour, it is important to use only fully ripened, flavourful tomatoes in this soup.

1 Place the tomatoes in a blender with the garlic and olive oil, if using. Blend until smooth.

2 Pass the mixture through a sieve (strainer) to remove the seeds. Stir in the balsamic vinegar and season to taste with black pepper. Leave in the refrigerator to chill.

3 Toast the bread lightly on both sides. While still hot, cut off the crusts and slice in half horizontally. Place the toast on a board with the uncooked sides facing down and, using a circular motion, rub to remove any doughy pieces of bread.

4 Cut each slice into 4 triangles. Place on a grill (broiler) pan and toast the uncooked sides until lightly golden. Garnish each bowl of soup with a spoonful of yogurt and serve with the Melba toast.

Avocado, Tomato and Mozzarella Pasta Salad with Pine Nuts

A salad made from ingredients representing the colours of the Italian flag – a sunny cheerful dish!

Serves 4

INGREDIENTS

175g/6oz/1½ cups pasta bows (farfalle)
6 ripe tomatoes
225g/8oz mozzarella cheese
1 large ripe avocado
30ml/2 tbsp pine nuts, toasted
1 fresh basil sprig, to garnish

DRESSING

90ml/6 tbsp olive oil
30ml/2 tbsp wine vinegar
5ml/1 tsp balsamic vinegar (optional)
5ml/1 tsp wholegrain mustard
pinch of sugar
30ml/2 tbsp chopped fresh basil
salt and ground black pepper

olive oil

avocado

tomatoes

basil

mozzarella cheese

pine nuts   *pasta bows*

1 Cook the pasta in plenty of boiling salted water according to the manufacturer's instructions. Drain well and cool.

2 Slice the tomatoes and mozzarella cheese into thin rounds.

3 Halve the avocado, remove the stone (pit) and peel off the skin. Slice the flesh lengthways.

4 Whisk all the dressing ingredients together in a small bowl.

5 Arrange the tomato, mozzarella and avocado in overlapping slices around the edge of a flat plate.

6 Toss the pasta with half the dressing and the chopped basil. Pile into the centre of the plate. Pour over the remaining dressing, sprinkle over the pine nuts and garnish with a sprig of fresh basil. Serve immediately.

Cucumber and Alfalfa Tortillas

Wheat tortillas are extremely simple to prepare at home. Served with a crisp, fresh salsa, they make a marvellous light lunch or supper dish.

COOK'S TIP
When peeling the avocado be sure to scrape off the bright green flesh from immediately under the skin as this gives the sauce its vivid green colour.

Serves 4

INGREDIENTS
225g/8oz/2 cups plain (all-purpose) flour
pinch of salt
45ml/3 tbsp olive oil
100–150ml/4–5fl oz/½–⅔ cup warm water
lime wedges, to garnish

FOR THE SALSA
1 red onion, finely chopped
1 fresh red chilli, seeded and finely chopped
30ml/2 tbsp chopped fresh dill or coriander (cilantro)
½ cucumber, peeled and chopped
175g/6oz alfalfa sprouts

FOR THE SAUCE
1 large avocado, peeled and stoned (pitted)
juice of 1 lime
25g/1oz/2 tbsp soft goat's cheese
pinch of paprika

avocado
goat's cheese
red chilli
cucumber
dill
alfalfa sprouts

1 Mix all the salsa ingredients together in a bowl and set aside.

2 To make the sauce, place the avocado, lime juice and goat's cheese in a food processor or blender and blend until smooth. Place in a bowl and cover with clear film (plastic wrap). Dust with paprika just before serving.

3 To make the tortillas, place the flour and salt in a food processor, add the oil and blend. Gradually add the water (the amount will vary depending on the type of flour). Stop adding water when a stiff dough has formed. Turn out on to a floured board and knead until smooth. Cover with a damp cloth.

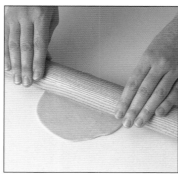

4 Divide the dough into 8 pieces. Knead each piece for a couple of minutes and form into a ball. Flatten and roll out each ball to a 23cm/9in circle.

5 Heat an ungreased heavy pan. Cook one tortilla at a time for about 30 seconds on each side. Place the cooked tortillas in a clean dish towel and repeat until you have 8 tortillas.

6 To serve, spread each tortilla with a spoonful of avocado sauce, top with salsa and roll up. Garnish with lime wedges.

Pear and Pecan Nut Salad with Blue Cheese Dressing

Toasted pecan nuts have a special union with crisp white pears. Their robust flavours combine especially well with a rich blue cheese dressing and make this a salad to remember.

Serves 4

INGREDIENTS
75g/3oz/½ cup shelled pecan nuts, roughly chopped
3 crisp pears
175g/6oz young spinach, stems removed
1 escarole or butterhead lettuce
1 radicchio
30ml/2 tbsp Blue Cheese and Chive Dressing
salt and ground black pepper
crusty bread, to serve

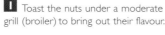
pears

pecan nuts

escarole

radicchio

spinach

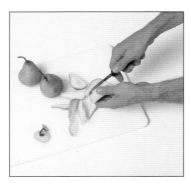

1 Toast the nuts under a moderate grill (broiler) to bring out their flavour.

2 Cut the pears into even slices, leaving the skin intact and discarding the cores.

3 Wash the salad leaves and spin dry. Add the pears together with the toasted pecans, then toss with the dressing. Distribute between 4 large plates and season with salt and black pepper. Serve with warm crusty bread.

Melon and Prosciutto Salad with Strawberry Salsa

Sections of cool fragrant melon wrapped with slices of air-dried ham make a delicious salad starter. If strawberries are in season, serve with a savoury-sweet strawberry salsa and watch it disappear.

Serves 4

INGREDIENTS
1 large cantaloupe, Galia or
    Charentais melon
175g/6oz prosciutto or Serrano
    ham, thinly sliced

SALSA
225g/8oz strawberries
5ml/1 tsp caster (superfine) sugar
30ml/2 tbsp groundnut (peanut) or
    sunflower oil
15ml/1 tbsp orange juice
½ tsp finely grated orange zest
½ tsp finely grated fresh root ginger
salt and ground black pepper

1 Halve the melon and take the seeds out with a spoon. Cut the rind away with a paring knife, then slice the melon thickly. Chill until ready to serve.

2 To make the salsa, hull the strawberries and cut them into large dice. Place in a small mixing bowl with the sugar and crush lightly to release the juices. Add the oil, orange juice, zest and ginger. Season with salt and a generous twist of black pepper.

3 Arrange the melon on a serving plate, lay the ham over the top and serve with a bowl of salsa.

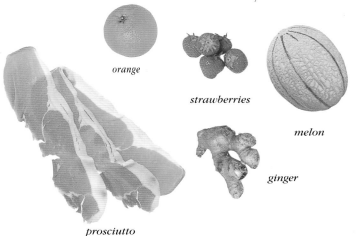

orange

strawberries

melon

ginger

prosciutto

Pasta with Prawns and Feta Cheese

This dish combines the richness of fresh prawns with the tartness of feta cheese. Goat's cheese could also be used.

Serves 4

INGREDIENTS
450g/1lb medium raw prawns
    (shrimp)
6 spring onions (scallions)
50g/2oz/4 tbsp butter
225g/8oz feta cheese
small bunch of fresh chives
450g/1lb/4 cups penne, garganelle
    or rigatoni
salt and ground black pepper

penne

spring onions

feta

chives

prawns

1 Remove the heads from the prawns by twisting and pulling off. Peel the prawns and discard the shells. Chop the spring onions.

2 Melt the butter in a pan and stir in the prawns. When they turn pink, add the spring onions and cook gently for 1 minute.

3 Cut the feta into 1cm/½in cubes.

4 Stir the feta cheese into the prawn mixture and season with black pepper.

5 Cut the chives into 2.5cm/1in lengths and stir half into the prawns.

6 Cook the pasta in plenty of boiling salted water according to the manufacturer's instructions. Drain well, pile into a warmed serving dish and top with the sauce. Sprinkle with the remaining chives and serve.

Chicken Goujons

Serve as a first course for eight people or as a filling main course for four. Delicious served with baby new potatoes and a green salad.

Serves 8

INGREDIENTS
4 boned and skinned chicken
    breast portions
175g/6oz/3 cups fresh breadcrumbs
5ml/1 tsp ground coriander
10ml/2 tsp ground paprika
2.5ml/½ tsp ground cumin
45ml/3 tbsp plain (all-purpose)
    flour
2 eggs, beaten
oil, for deep-frying
salt and ground black pepper
lemon slices and fresh coriander
    (cilantro) sprigs, to garnish

FOR THE DIP
300ml/½ pint/1¼ cups Greek
    (US strained plain) yogurt
30ml/2 tbsp lemon juice
60ml/4 tbsp chopped fresh coriander
    (cilantro)
60ml/4 tbsp chopped fresh parsley

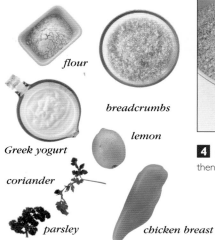

flour

breadcrumbs

Greek yogurt

lemon

coriander

parsley   *chicken breast*

eggs

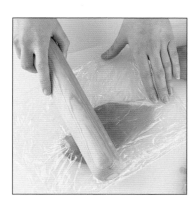

1 Divide the chicken breasts into two natural fillets. Place them between two sheets of clear film (plastic wrap) and, using a rolling pin, flatten each one to a thickness of 5mm/¼in.

2 Cut into diagonal 2.5cm/1in strips.

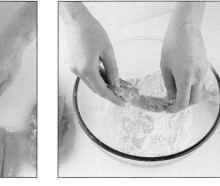

3 Mix the breadcrumbs with the spices and seasoning. Toss the chicken fillet pieces (goujons) in the flour, keeping them separate.

4 Dip the fillets into the beaten egg and then coat in the breadcrumb mixture.

5 Thoroughly mix all the ingredients for the dip together, and season to taste. Chill until required.

6 Heat the oil in a heavy pan. It is ready for deep-frying when a piece of bread tossed into the oil sizzles on the surface. Fry the goujons in batches until golden and crisp. Drain on kitchen paper and keep warm in the oven until all the chicken has been fried. Garnish with lemon slices and sprigs of fresh coriander.

FISH AND SHELLFISH

Fillets of Pink Trout with Tarragon Cream Sauce

If you do not like the idea of cooking and serving trout on the bone, ask your fishmonger to fillet and skin the fish. Serve two fillets per person.

VARIATION
This recipe can also be made with salmon fillets, and the dry sherry may be substituted with white wine.

Serves 4

INGREDIENTS
25g/1oz/2 tbsp butter
4 fresh trout, filleted and skinned
salt and ground black pepper
new potatoes and runner (green)
  beans, to serve

FOR THE CREAM SAUCE
2 large spring onions (scallions),
  white part only, chopped
½ cucumber, peeled, seeded and
  cut into short batons
5ml/1 tsp cornflour (cornstarch)
150ml/¼ pint/⅔ cup single (light)
  cream
50ml/2fl oz/¼ cup dry sherry
30ml/2 tbsp chopped fresh tarragon
1 tomato, seeded and chopped

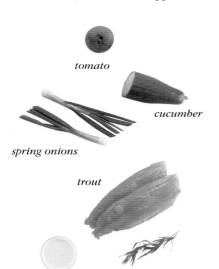

tomato

cucumber

spring onions

trout

cream   tarragon

1 Melt the butter in a large frying pan, season the trout fillets and cook for 6 minutes, turning once. Transfer to a plate, cover and keep warm.

2 To make the sauce, add the spring onions and cucumber to the pan, and cook over a gentle heat, stirring, until soft but not coloured.

3 Remove the pan from the heat and stir in the cornflour.

4 Return to the heat and pour in the cream and sherry. Simmer to thicken, stirring continuously.

5 Add the chopped tarragon and tomato, and season to taste.

6 Spoon the sauce over the fillets and serve with buttered new potatoes and runner beans.

Prawn Salad with Curry Dressing

Curry spices add an unexpected twist to this salad. Warm flavours combine especially well with sweet prawns and grated apple.

Serves 4

INGREDIENTS
1 ripe tomato
½ iceberg lettuce, shredded
1 small onion
1 small bunch fresh coriander
  (cilantro)
15ml/1 tbsp lemon juice
450g/1lb cooked peeled prawns
  (shrimp)
1 apple, peeled
salt

DRESSING
75ml/5 tbsp mayonnaise
5ml/1 tsp mild curry paste
15ml/1 tbsp tomato ketchup

TO DECORATE
8 whole prawns (shrimp)
8 lemon wedges
4 fresh coriander (cilantro) sprigs

1 To peel the tomato, pierce the skin with a knife and immerse in boiling water for 20 seconds. Drain and cool under running water. Peel off the skin. Halve the tomato, push the seeds out with your thumb and discard them. Cut the flesh into large dice.

tomato   apple

coriander

lemon

onion

prawns

2 Finely shred the lettuce, onion and coriander. Add the tomato, moisten with lemon juice and season with salt.

3 To make the dressing, combine the mayonnaise, curry paste and tomato ketchup in a small bowl. Add 30ml/2tbsp water to thin the dressing and season to taste with salt.

4 Combine the prawns with the dressing. Quarter and core the apple and grate into the mixture.

COOK'S TIP

Fresh coriander (cilantro) is inclined to wilt if kept out of water. Keep it in a jar of water in the refrigerator covered with a plastic bag and it will stay fresh for several days.

5 Distribute the shredded lettuce mixture between 4 plates or bowls. Pile the prawn mixture in the centre of each and decorate with 2 whole prawns, 2 lemon wedges and a sprig of coriander.

Fillets of Hake Baked with Thyme and Garlic

Quick cooking is the essence of this dish. Use the freshest garlic available and half the amount of dried thyme if fresh is not available.

Serves 4

INGREDIENTS
1 shallot, finely chopped
2 garlic cloves, thinly sliced
4 fresh thyme sprigs, plus extra, to garnish
4 hake fillets, about 175g/6oz each
grated rind and juice of 1 lemon, plus extra juice, for drizzling
30ml/2 tbsp extra virgin olive oil
salt and ground black pepper

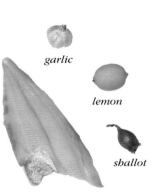

garlic

lemon

shallot

bake fillet

thyme

1 Preheat the oven to 180°C/350°F/Gas 4. Lay the hake fillets in the base of a large roasting pan. Sprinkle the shallot, garlic cloves and thyme on top.

2 Season well with salt and pepper.

3 Drizzle over the lemon juice and oil. Bake for about 15 minutes. Serve sprinkled with finely grated lemon rind and garnished with thyme sprigs.

VARIATION

If hake is not available you can use cod or haddock fillets for this recipe. You can also use a mixture of fresh herbs rather than just thyme.

Stuffed Sardines

This Middle Eastern-inspired dish doesn't take a lot of preparation and is a meal in itself. Just serve with a crisp green salad tossed in a fresh lemon vinaigrette to make it complete.

Serves 4

INGREDIENTS
900g/2lb fresh sardines
30ml/2 tbsp olive oil
75g/3oz/½ cup wholemeal
 (whole-wheat) breadcrumbs
50g/2oz/¼ cup sultanas (golden
 raisins)
50g/2oz/½ cup pine nuts
50g/2oz canned anchovy fillets,
 drained
60ml/4 tbsp chopped fresh parsley
1 onion, finely chopped
salt and ground black pepper
lemon wedges, to garnish

sultanas

pine nuts

onion

sardines

olive oil

bread

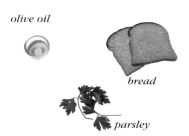

parsley

1 Preheat the oven to 200°C/400°F/ Gas 6. Gut the sardines and wipe out thoroughly with kitchen paper. Heat the oil in a frying pan and fry the breadcrumbs until golden.

2 Add the sultanas, pine nuts, anchovies, parsley, onion and seasoning and mix well.

3 Stuff each sardine with the mixture. Close the fish firmly and place closely packed together in an ovenproof dish.

4 Sprinkle any remaining filling over the sardines and drizzle with olive oil. Bake for 30 minutes and serve garnished with fresh lemon wedges.

Salmon with Spicy Pesto

This is a great way to bone salmon steaks to give a solid piece of fish. It's also cheaper than buying fillet, when you are paying for the fishmonger to bone it. The pesto is unusual because it uses sunflower kernels and chilli as its flavouring rather than the classic basil and pine nuts.

Serves 4

INGREDIENTS
4 salmon steaks, about 225g/8oz
  each
30ml/2 tbsp sunflower oil
finely grated rind and juice of 1 lime
salt and ground black pepper

FOR THE PESTO
6 mild fresh red chillies
2 garlic cloves
30ml/2 tbsp pumpkin or sunflower
  seeds
finely grated rind and juice of 1 lime
75ml/5 tbsp olive oil

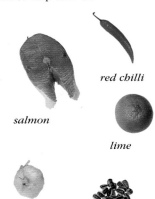

salmon

red chilli

lime

garlic

pumpkin seeds

1 Insert a very sharp knife close to the top of the bone. Working closely to the bone, cut your way to the end of the steak so one side of the steak has been released and one side is still attached. Repeat with the other side. Pull out any extra visible bones with a pair of tweezers.

2 Sprinkle a little salt on the surface and take hold of the end of the salmon piece skin-side down. Insert a small sharp knife under the skin and, working away from you, cut off the skin keeping as close to the skin as possible. Repeat with the other pieces of fish.

5 For the pesto, de-seed the chillies, and place them together with the garlic cloves, pumpkin seeds, lime juice, rind and seasoning into a food processor fitted with a metal blade. Process until well mixed. Pour the olive oil gradually over the moving blades until the sauce has thickened and emulsified. Drain the salmon from its marinade. Grill (broil) the fish steaks for 5 minutes either side and serve with the spicy pesto.

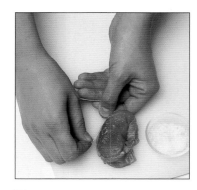

3 Wrap each piece of fish into a circle, with the thinner end wrapped around the fatter end. Secure tightly with a length of string.

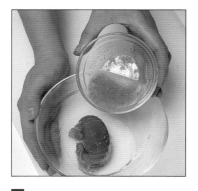

4 Rub the sunflower oil into the boneless fish rounds. Add the lime juice and rind and marinate in the refrigerator for 2 hours.

Fish Curry

Any mixture of white fish works well with this fresh-tasting curry. Serve with warm naan bread to mop up the delicious juices.

Serves 4

INGREDIENTS

675g/1½lb white boneless fish such
    as halibut, cod, coley or monkfish
juice of ½ lime
5ml/2 tsp cider vinegar
225g/8oz/4 cups grated fresh
    coconut
2.5cm/1in piece fresh root ginger,
    peeled and grated
6 garlic cloves
450g/1lb tomatoes, chopped
45ml/3 tbsp sunflower oil
350g/12oz onions, roughly chopped
20 curry leaves
5ml/1 tsp ground coriander
2.5ml/½ tsp ground turmeric
10ml/2 tsp ground chilli
2.5ml/½ tsp fenugreek seeds
2.5ml/½ tsp cumin seeds
salt and ground black pepper
lime slices, to garnish
banana leaves, to serve

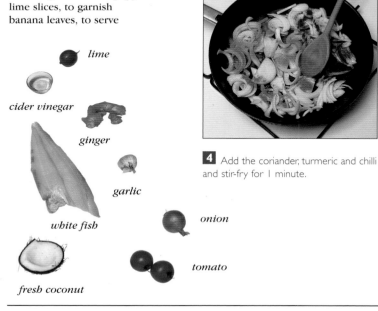

lime

cider vinegar

ginger

garlic

white fish

onion

tomato

fresh coconut

1 Marinate the fish in lime juice, vinegar and a pinch of salt for 30 minutes.

2 In a food processor fitted with a metal blade, process the grated coconut, ginger, garlic cloves and tomatoes to make a paste.

3 Heat the oil in a frying pan, add the onions and cook until golden brown, then add the curry leaves.

4 Add the coriander, turmeric and chilli and stir-fry for 1 minute.

5 Add the coconut paste and cook for 3–4 minutes, stirring constantly. Pour in 300ml/½ pint/1¼ cups water, bring to the boil, and simmer for 4 minutes.

6 Pound the fenugreek and cumin seeds together in a pestle and mortar. Lay the fish on top of the simmering sauce, sprinkle over the fenugreek mixture and cook for 15 minutes or until the fish is tender. Serve on banana leaves and garnish with lime slices.

Halibut with Fresh Tomato and Basil Salsa

Take care when cooking this dish as the fish tends to break up very easily, especially as the skin has been removed. Season well to bring out the delicate flavour of the halibut and the fresh taste of the sauce.

Serves 4

INGREDIENTS
4 halibut fillets, about 175g/6oz
   each
45ml/3 tbsp olive oil
salt and ground black pepper

FOR THE SALSA
1 medium tomato, roughly chopped
¼ red onion, finely chopped
1 small jalapeño pepper
30ml/2 tbsp balsamic vinegar
10 large fresh basil leaves
15ml/1 tbsp olive oil

tomato

jalapeño pepper

halibut fillet

basil

red onion

1 In a bowl mix together the tomato, red onion, jalapeño pepper and balsamic vinegar.

2 Slice the basil leaves finely.

3 Stir the basil and the olive oil into the tomato mixture. Season to taste. Cover and leave to marinate for at least 3 hours.

4 For the fish, rub the halibut fillets with olive oil and seasoning. Heat a grill (broiler) or barbecue and cook for about 4 minutes either side, depending on the thickness of each fillet. Baste with olive oil as necessary. Serve with the salsa.

Cod and Spinach Parcels

The best way to serve this dish is to slice each parcel into about four and reveal the meaty large flakes of white fish. Drizzle the sauce over the slices.

Serves 4

INGREDIENTS
4 pieces of thick cod fillet, about
    175g/6oz each, skinned
225g/8oz large spinach leaves
2.5g/½ tsp freshly ground nutmeg
45ml/3 tbsp white wine
salt and ground black pepper

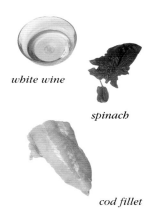

white wine

spinach

cod fillet

1 Preheat the oven to 180°C/350°F/ Gas 4. Season the fish well with salt and ground black pepper.

2 Blanch the spinach leaves in boiling water for a minute and refresh under cold water.

3 Pat the spinach leaves dry on absorbent kitchen paper.

4 Wrap the spinach around each fish fillet. Sprinkle with nutmeg. Place in a roasting pan, pour over the wine and poach for 15 minutes. Slice and serve hot.

San Francisco Salad

California is a salad-maker's paradise and is renowned for the healthiness of its produce. San Francisco has become the salad capital of California, although this recipe is based on a salad served at the Chez Panisse restaurant in Berkeley.

Serves 4

INGREDIENTS

900g/2lb langoustines, Dublin
    Bay prawns (jumbo shrimp)
    or Danish lobster
1 fennel bulb, about 50g/2oz, sliced
2 ripe medium tomatoes, quartered,
    and 4 small tomatoes
30ml/2 tbsp olive oil, plus extra, for
    moistening the salad leaves
60ml/4 tbsp brandy
150ml/5fl oz/⅔ cup dry white wine
200ml/7floz can lobster or crab
    bisque
30ml/2 tbsp chopped fresh tarragon
45ml/3 tbsp double (heavy) cream
225g/8oz green beans, trimmed
2 oranges
175g/6oz lamb's lettuce
125g/4oz rocket (arugula)
½ frisée lettuce
salt and cayenne pepper

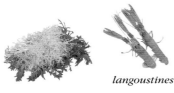

langoustines

frisée lettuce

orange

tomatoes
fennel

lamb's lettuce
rocket

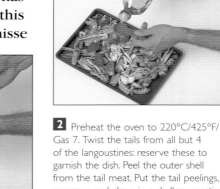

1 Bring a large pan of salted water to the boil, add the langoustines and simmer for 10 minutes. Refresh under cold running water.

2 Preheat the oven to 220°C/425°F/Gas 7. Twist the tails from all but 4 of the langoustines: reserve these to garnish the dish. Peel the outer shell from the tail meat. Put the tail peelings, carapace and claws in a shallow roasting pan with the fennel and tomatoes. Toss with the oil and roast near the top of the oven for 20 minutes to bring out the flavours.

3 Remove the roasting pan from the oven and place it over a moderate heat on top of the stove. Add the brandy and ignite to release the flavour of the alcohol. Add the wine and simmer briefly.

4 Transfer the contents of the roasting pan to a food processor and reduce to a coarse purée: this will take only 10–15 seconds. Rub the purée through a fine nylon sieve (strainer) into a bowl. Add the lobster bisque, tarragon and cream. Season to taste with salt and a little cayenne pepper.

5 Bring a pan of salted water to the boil and cook the beans for 6 minutes. Drain and cool under running water. To segment the oranges, cut the peel from the top and bottom, and then from the sides, with a serrated knife. Loosen the segments by cutting between the membranes and the flesh.

6 Wash and spin the salad leaves. Moisten with olive oil and distribute between 4 serving plates. Fold the langoustine tails into the dressing and distribute between the plates. Add the beans, orange segments and small tomatoes, decorate each plate with a whole langoustine and serve warm.

Vietnamese Stuffed Squid

The smaller the squid the sweeter the dish will taste. Be very careful not to overcook the flesh as it becomes tough very quickly.

Serves 4

INGREDIENTS
6 small squid, cleaned
50g/2oz cellophane noodles
30ml/2 tbsp groundnut (peanut) oil
2 spring onions (scallions), finely
   chopped
8 shiitake mushrooms, halved
   if large
250g/9oz minced (ground) pork
1 garlic clove, chopped
30ml/2 tbsp Thai fish sauce
5ml/1 tsp caster (superfine) sugar
15ml/1 tbsp finely chopped fresh
   coriander (cilantro)
5ml/1 tsp lemon juice
salt and ground black pepper

noodles

fresh coriander

garlic

squid

minced pork

spring onion

shiitake mushrooms

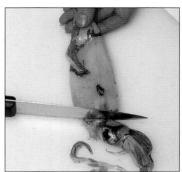

1 Preheat the oven to 200°C/400°F/ Gas 6. Clean the squid and remove any excess membrane and tentacles.

2 Put the noodles into a pan of boiling water. Remove the pan from the heat and soak the noodles for 20 minutes.

3 Heat 15ml/1 tbsp of the oil in a wok and stir-fry the spring onions, mushrooms, pork and garlic for 4 minutes until the meat is golden.

4 Add the noodles, fish sauce, sugar, seasoning, coriander and lemon juice.

5 Stuff the squid two-thirds full with the mixture and secure with saté or cocktail sticks (toothpicks). Drizzle over the remaining oil, prick the squid twice and bake in the preheated oven for 10 minutes. Serve hot.

Classic Whole Salmon

Serving a boneless whole salmon is a delight. Take care when cooking the fish. If you own a fish kettle the method is slightly different. Cover with water, add a dash of white wine, a bay leaf, sliced lemon and black peppercorns and bring to the boil for 6 minutes. Leave to cool completely in the water until cold. Drain, pat dry, and continue as instructed in the recipe.

Serves 8

INGREDIENTS
1 whole salmon
300ml/½ pint/1¼ cups water
150ml/¼ pint/⅔ cup white wine
3 bay leaves
1 lemon, sliced
12 black peppercorns
2 cucumbers, thinly sliced
mixed fresh herbs such as parsley,
   chervil and chives, to garnish
mayonnaise, to serve

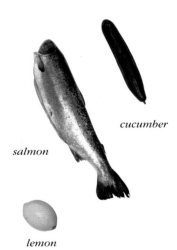

cucumber

salmon

lemon

bay leaves

1 Preheat the oven to 180°C/350°F/ Gas 4. Clean the inside of the salmon, making sure all the gut has been removed and the inside cavity has been well wiped out with kitchen paper. Cut the tail into a neat "V" shape with a sharp pair of scissors. Place the fish on a large piece of double thickness foil. Lay the bay leaves, sliced lemon and black peppercorns inside the cavity. Wrap the foil around and up the sides, and pour over the water and wine. Seal the parcel and place in a large roasting pan.

2 Bake in the preheated oven, allowing 15 minutes per pound plus 15 minutes extra. Remove from the oven, open up the parcel and leave to cool. Don't leave to chill overnight as the fish-skin will be impossible to remove the next day.

3 Cut off the head and tail, reserving them if you want them to display the fish later. Turn the fish upside-down on to a board so the flattest side is uppermost. Carefully peel off the base foil and the skin. Using a sharp knife, scrap away any excess brown flesh from the pink salmon flesh.

4 Make an incision down the back fillet, drawing the flesh away from the central bone. Take one fillet and place on the serving dish. Remove the second fillet and place it beside the first to form the base of the fish.

5 Remove the central backbone from the fish.

6 Place the other half of the fish with the skin still intact, flesh-side down on top of the base fish. Peel off the upper skin and any brown bits. Replace the head and tail if required. Lay the cucumber slices on top of the fish, working from the tail end, resembling scales, until all the flesh is covered. Garnish the plate with large bunches of fresh herbs and serve with mayonnaise.

Salmon Coulibiac

A complicated Russian dish that takes a lot of preparation, but is well worth it. Traditionally sturgeon is used but as this is difficult to get hold of salmon may be substituted. As a special treat serve with shots of vodka for an authentic Russian flavour.

Serves 8

INGREDIENTS
2 eggs, separated
750ml/1¼ pints/3 cups milk
225g/8oz/2 cups plain (all-purpose) flour
350g/12oz/1½ cups butter, melted
2.5ml/½ tsp salt
2.5ml/½ tsp caster (superfine) sugar
450g/1lb puff pastry
1 egg, beaten
salt and ground black pepper

FOR THE FILLING
50g/2oz/4 tbsp butter
350g/12oz chestnut mushrooms, sliced
100ml/3½fl oz/½ cup white wine
juice of ½ lemon
675g/1½lb salmon fillet, skinned
115g/4oz/½ cup long grain rice
1 large onion, chopped
30ml/2 tbsp chopped fresh dill, plus extra sprigs, to garnish
4 hard-boiled eggs, shelled and sliced, plus extra wedges, to garnish

salmon fillet
puff pastry
dill
rice
onion
lemon
chestnut mushrooms
milk
egg
butter

1 For the pancakes, whisk the egg yolks together and add the milk. Gradually beat in the flour, 335g/11½oz of the melted butter, the salt and sugar until smooth. Leave to stand for 30 minutes.

2 Whisk the egg whites until they just form stiff peaks, then fold into the batter. Heat the remaining butter in a heavy frying pan and add about 45ml/3 tbsp of the batter. Turn and cook until golden. Repeat until all the mixture has been used up, brushing on a little melted butter when stacking the pancakes. When they are cool, cut into long rectangles and cover until ready to use.

3 For the filling, melt the butter in a large frying pan. Add the mushrooms and cook for 3 minutes. Add 60ml/4 tbsp of the wine and boil for 2 minutes, then lower the heat and simmer for a further 5 minutes. Add the remaining wine and lemon juice.

4 Place the salmon on top of the cooked mushrooms, cover with foil, and gently steam for 8–10 minutes until just cooked. Remove the salmon from the pan and set aside.

5 With a slotted spoon, transfer the mushrooms to a bowl. Pour the cooking liquid into a large pan. Add the rice and cook for 10–15 minutes, until tender, adding water or more wine if necessary. Remove from the heat and stir in the dill and seasoning. Melt the remaining butter and fry the onion until brown. Set aside.

6 Grease and flour a large baking sheet. Using baking parchment, cut out a fish-shaped template that will fit easily on the baking sheet. Roll out just less than half the pastry and use the template to cut a fish shape. Place on the baking sheet. Leaving the edges clear, spread out half the pancakes on the pastry and top with half the mushrooms, half the rice mixture, half the onion, and half the hard-boiled egg. Place the salmon on top, cutting to fit if necessary.

7 Finish the layering process in reverse. Roll out the remaining pastry and cut out a slightly larger fish shape than before, so that it will cover the filling. Brush the base pastry rim with beaten egg, fit the pastry top in place and seal the edges. Chill for 1 hour.

8 Preheat the oven to 220°C/425°F/Gas 7. Cut four small slits in the top of the pastry, brush with more egg and bake for 10 minutes. Reduce the oven temperature to 190°C/375°F/Gas 5 and bake for 30 minutes more, until golden. Garnish with fresh dill sprigs and wedges of hard-boiled egg, and serve.

Tuscan Tuna and Beans

A great store-cupboard dish which is especially good for children as it contains no bones.

Serves 4

INGREDIENTS
1 red onion, finely chopped
30ml/2 tbsp smooth French mustard
300ml/½ pint/1¼ cups olive oil
60ml/4 tbsp white wine vinegar
30ml/2 tbsp chopped fresh parsley,
    plus extra to garnish
30ml/2 tbsp chopped fresh chives
30ml/2 tbsp chopped fresh
    tarragon or chervil
400g/14oz can haricot beans
400g/14oz can kidney beans
225g/8oz canned tuna in oil,
    drained and lightly flaked

kidney beans

mustard

chives

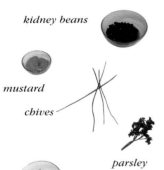
haricot beans

parsley

tuna

red onion

tarragon

1 Chop the onion finely.

2 In a small bowl, beat the mustard, oil, vinegar, parsley, chives and tarragon or chervil together.

3 Drain the canned beans.

4 Mix the red onion, beans and dressing together thoroughly, toss well and serve.

Grilled Sea Bream with Fennel, Mustard and Orange

Sea bream is a revelation to anyone unfamiliar with its creamy, rich flavour. The fish has a firm white flesh that partners well with a rich butter sauce, sharpened here with a dash of frozen orange juice concentrate.

Serves 2

INGREDIENTS
2 baking potatoes
2 sea bream, about 350g/12oz each, scaled and gutted
10ml/2 tsp Dijon mustard
5ml/1 tsp fennel seeds
30ml/2 tbsp olive oil
50g/2oz watercress
175g/6oz mixed lettuce leaves, such as frisée or lamb's lettuce

FOR THE SAUCE
30ml/2 tbsp frozen orange juice concentrate
175g/6oz/¾ cup unsalted (sweet) butter, diced
salt and cayenne pepper

COOK'S TIP

For speedy baked potatoes, microwave small potatoes on 100%/ HIGH power for 8 minutes, then crisp in a hot oven preheated to 200°C/ 400°F/Gas 6 for a further 10 minutes. Split, butter and serve.

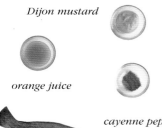

Dijon mustard

orange juice

cayenne pepper

lettuce

sea bream

1 Cook the potatoes according to the tip at the beginning of this recipe. Preheat a moderate grill (broiler). Slash the bream four times on either side. Combine the mustard and fennel seeds, then spread over both sides of the fish. Moisten with oil and grill (broil) for 12 minutes, turning once.

2 Place the orange juice concentrate in a bowl and heat over 2.5cm/1 in of boiling water. Remove the pan from the heat, and gradually whisk in the butter until creamy. Season, cover and set aside.

3 Moisten the watercress and lettuce leaves with the remaining olive oil, arrange the fish on two large plates and put the leaves to one side. Spoon over the sauce and serve with the potatoes.

Barbecued Salmon with Red Onion Marmalade

Salmon barbecues well but make sure it is at least 2.5cm/1in thick to make it easy to turn when cooking. The red onion marmalade is rich and delicious, and complements the simply cooked fish perfectly.

Serves 4

INGREDIENTS
4 salmon steaks, cut 2.5cm/1in thick, no thinner
30ml/2 tbsp olive oil
salt and ground black pepper

FOR THE RED ONION MARMALADE
5 medium red onions, peeled
50g/2oz/4 tbsp butter
175ml/6fl oz/³⁄₄ cup red wine vinegar
50ml/2fl oz/¹⁄₄ cup crème de cassis or 15ml/1 tbsp puréed blackcurrants, fresh or canned
50ml/2fl oz/¹⁄₄ cup grenadine
50ml/2fl oz/¹⁄₄ cup red wine

red wine

salmon

red onion

butter

1 Rub the olive oil into the fish flesh.

2 Season the fish well with salt and pepper.

3 Finely slice the onions.

4 Melt the butter in a large heavy pan and add the onions. Sauté for 5 minutes.

5 Stir in the vinegar, cassis or puréed blackcurrants, grenadine and wine and continue to cook until the liquid has reduced. After about 10 minutes the liquid should have almost entirely evaporated and the onions will be glazed. Season well.

6 Brush the fish with a little more oil, and barbecue or griddle for 4 minutes on either side.

Poached Skate and Black Butter

Skate is one of those fish which actually improves after storing for a couple of days in the refrigerator. The capers in this dish can be omitted, leaving the simple burnt butter flavour standing on its own.

Serves 4

INGREDIENTS
1 litre/1¾ pints/4½ cups water
1 carrot, sliced
1 small onion, sliced
bouquet garni
6 peppercorns
120ml/4fl oz/½ cup white wine
  vinegar
5ml/1 tsp salt
8 skate wings

FOR THE BLACK BUTTER
115g/4oz/½ cup butter
30ml/2 tbsp drained capers

onion

peppercorns

carrot

butter

skate wings

bouquet garni

1 Place the water, carrot, onion, bouquet garni, peppercorns and 75ml/ 3fl oz/½ cup white wine vinegar and salt into a large, heavy pan. Bring to the boil and simmer uncovered for 20 minutes.

2 Poach the skate wings in the liquid for about 10 minutes. Drain and keep warm, reserving the fish stock for another use if you wish.

3 Meanwhile, make the black butter. Heat the butter in a pan until it turns brown. Remove from the heat and stir in the capers.

4 Pour the butter over the skate, then deglaze the pan with the remaining vinegar and pour on top.

Thick Cod Fillet with Fresh Mixed-herb Crust

Mixed fresh herbs make this a delicious crust. Season well and serve with large lemon wedges.

Serves 4

INGREDIENTS
25g/1oz/2 tbsp butter
15ml/1 tbsp fresh chervil
15ml/1 tbsp fresh parsley
15ml/1 tbsp fresh chives
175g/6oz/3 cups wholemeal
  (whole-wheat) breadcrumbs
4 thickly cut cod fillets, about
  225g/8oz each, skinned
15ml/1 tbsp olive oil
salt and ground black pepper
lemon wedges, to garnish

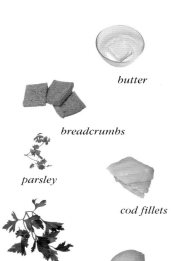

butter

breadcrumbs

parsley

cod fillets

chervil

lemon

1 Preheat the oven to 200°C/400°F/ Gas 6. Melt the butter and chop the herbs finely.

2 Mix the butter with the breadcrumbs, herbs and seasoning.

3 Press a quarter of the mixture on top of each fillet. Place on a baking sheet and drizzle over the olive oil. Bake for 15 minutes, until the fish flesh is firm and the top turns golden. Serve garnished with lemon wedges.

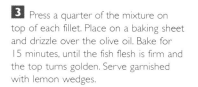

Turkey Tonnato

This low-fat version of the Italian dish 'vitello tonnato' is garnished with fine strips of red pepper instead of the traditional anchovy fillets.

Serves 4

INGREDIENTS
450g/1lb turkey fillets
1 small onion, sliced
1 bay leaf
4 black peppercorns
350ml/12fl oz/1½ cups
    chicken stock
200g/7oz can tuna in brine, drained
75ml/5 tbsp reduced-calorie
    mayonnaise
30ml/2 tbsp lemon juice
2 red (bell) peppers, seeded and
    thinly sliced
about 25 capers, drained
pinch of salt
mixed salad and tomatoes, to serve

tuna

lemon

onion

bay leaf

capers

mayonnaise

pepper

turkey fillet

stock

1 Put the turkey fillets in a single layer in a large, heavy pan. Add the onion, bay leaf, peppercorns and stock. Bring to the boil and reduce the heat. Cover and simmer for 12 minutes, or until tender.

2 Turn off the heat and leave the turkey to cool in the stock, then remove with a slotted spoon. Slice thickly and arrange on a serving plate.

3 Boil the stock until reduced to about 75ml/5 tbsp. Strain and leave to cool.

4 Put the tuna, mayonnaise, lemon juice, 45ml/3 tbsp of the reduced stock and salt into a blender or food processor and purée until smooth.

5 Stir in enough of the remaining stock to reduce the sauce to the thickness of double (heavy) cream. Spoon over the turkey.

6 Arrange the strips of red pepper in a lattice pattern over the turkey. Put a caper in the centre of each square. Chill in the refrigerator for 1 hour and serve with a fresh mixed salad and tomatoes.

Rockburger Salad with Sesame Croûtons

This salad plays on the ingredients that make up the all-American beefburger in a sesame bun. Inside the burger is a special layer of Roquefort, a blue ewe's-milk cheese from France.

Serves 4

INGREDIENTS
900g/2lb lean minced (ground) beef
1 egg
1 medium onion, finely chopped
10ml/2 tsp French mustard
½ tsp celery salt
125g/4oz Roquefort or other blue cheese
1 large sesame seed loaf
45ml/3 tbsp olive oil, preferably Spanish
1 small iceberg lettuce
50g/2oz rocket (arugula) or watercress
125ml/4fl oz French Dressing
4 ripe tomatoes, quartered
4 large spring onions (scallions), sliced
salt and ground black pepper

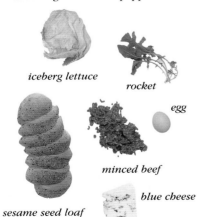

iceberg lettuce

rocket

egg

minced beef

blue cheese

sesame seed loaf

COOK'S TIP
If you're planning ahead, it's a good idea to freeze the filled burgers between pieces of waxed paper. They will keep in the freezer for up to 8 weeks.

1 Place the minced beef, egg, onion, mustard, celery salt and pepper in a mixing bowl. Combine thoroughly. Divide the mixture into 16 portions, each weighing 50g/2oz.

2 Flatten the pieces between 2 sheets of clear film (plastic wrap) or baking parchment to form 13cm/5in rounds.

3 Place 15g/½oz of the cheese on each of 8 of the thin burgers. Sandwich with the other 8 and press the edges together firmly. Store between pieces of clear film or baking parchment, and chill until ready to cook.

4 To make the sesame croûtons, preheat the grill (broiler) to a moderate temperature. Remove the sesame crust from the bread, then cut the crust into short fingers. Moisten with olive oil and toast evenly for 10–15 minutes.

5 Season the burgers and grill (broil) for 10 minutes, turning once.

6 Wash the salad leaves and spin dry. Toss with the dressing, then distribute between 4 large plates. Place 2 rockburgers in the centre of each plate and the tomatoes, spring onions and sesame croûtons around the edge.

Frankfurter Salad with Mustard and Caraway Dressing

A last-minute salad you can throw together using store-cupboard ingredients.

Serves 4

INGREDIENTS
700g/1½lb small new potatoes, scrubbed or scraped
2 eggs
350g/12oz frankfurters
1 round (butterhead) or Batavia lettuce
225g/8oz young spinach, stems removed
salt and ground black pepper

DRESSING
45ml/3 tbsp safflower oil
30ml/2 tbsp olive oil, preferably Spanish
15ml/1 tbsp white wine vinegar
10ml/2 tsp mustard
5ml/1 tsp caraway seeds, crushed

1 Bring the potatoes to the boil in salted water and simmer for 20 minutes. Drain, cover and keep warm. Hard-boil the eggs for 12 minutes. Refresh in cold water, shell and cut into quarters.

2 Score the frankfurter skins corkscrew-fashion with a small knife, then cover with boiling water and simmer for about 5 minutes to heat through. Drain well, cover and keep warm.

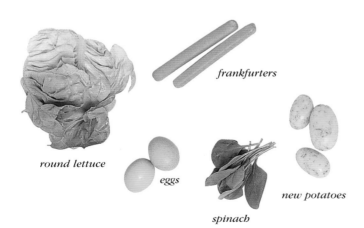

frankfurters

round lettuce

eggs

spinach

new potatoes

3 Combine the dressing ingredients in a screw-top jar and shake.

4 Wash and spin the salad leaves, moisten with half of the dressing and distribute between 4 large plates.

5 Moisten the potatoes and frankfurters with the remainder of the dressing and arrange on the salad.

6 Finish with sections of hard-boiled egg, season and serve.

COOK'S TIP

Mustard has an important place in the salad-maker's cupboard. Varieties differ from country to country and often suggest particular flavours. This salad has a German slant to it and calls for a sweet-and-sour German-style mustard. American mustards have a similar quality.

Veal Escalopes with Artichokes

Artichokes are very hard to prepare fresh, so use canned artichoke hearts instead – they have an excellent flavour and are simple to use.

Serves 4

INGREDIENTS
450g/1lb veal escalopes (scallops)
1 shallot
115g/4oz smoked bacon,
  finely chopped
1 × 400g/14oz can artichoke hearts
  in brine, drained and quartered
150ml/¼ pint/⅔ cup veal stock
3 fresh rosemary sprigs
60ml/4 tbsp double (heavy) cream
salt and ground black pepper
fresh rosemary sprigs, to garnish

veal escalopes

double cream

artichoke hearts

1 Cut the veal into thin slices.

2 Using a sharp knife, cut the shallot into thin slices.

3 Heat the wok, then add the bacon. Stir-fry for 2 minutes. When the fat is released, add the veal and shallot and stir-fry for 3–4 minutes.

4 Add the artichokes and stir-fry for 1 minute. Stir in the stock and rosemary and simmer for 2 minutes. Stir in the double cream, season with salt and pepper and serve garnished with sprigs of fresh rosemary.

Stir-fried Duck with Blueberries

Serve this conveniently quick dinner party dish with sprigs of fresh mint, which will give a wonderful fresh aroma as you bring the meal to the table.

Serves 4

INGREDIENTS
2 duck breasts, about 175g/6oz each
30ml/2 tbsp sunflower oil
15ml/1 tbsp red wine vinegar
5ml/1 tsp sugar
5ml/1 tsp red wine
5ml/1 tsp *crème de cassis*
115g/4oz fresh blueberries
15ml/1 tbsp chopped fresh mint
salt and ground black pepper
fresh mint sprigs, to garnish

duck

red wine vinegar

blueberries

red wine

mint

1 Cut the duck breasts into neat slices. Season well with salt and pepper.

2 Heat the wok, then add the oil. When the oil is hot, stir-fry the duck for 3 minutes.

3 Add the red wine vinegar, sugar, red wine and *crème de cassis*. Bubble for 3 minutes, to reduce to a thick syrup.

4 Stir in the blueberries, sprinkle over the mint and serve garnished with sprigs of fresh mint.

Pan-fried Pork with Peaches and Green Peppercorns

When peaches are in season, consider this speedy pork dish, brought alive with green peppercorns.

Serves 4

INGREDIENTS
400g/14oz/2 cups long grain rice
1 litre/1¾ pints/4 cups chicken stock
4 pork chops or loin pieces, about
    200g/7oz each
30ml/2 tbsp vegetable oil
30ml/2 tbsp dark rum or sherry
1 small onion, chopped
3 large ripe peaches
15ml/1 tbsp green peppercorns
15ml/1 tbsp white wine vinegar
salt and ground black pepper

onion

pork chops

dark rum

oil

green peppercorns

white wine vinegar

peaches

VARIATION
If peaches are not ripe when picked, they can be difficult to peel. Only tree-ripened fruit is suitable for peeling. If fresh peaches are out of season, a can of sliced peaches may be used instead.

1 Cover the rice with 900ml/1½ pints/ 3¾ cups chicken stock. Stir, bring to a simmer and cook uncovered for 15 minutes. Switch off the heat and cover for 5 minutes. Season the pork with a generous twist of black pepper. Heat a large bare metal frying pan and moisten the pork with 15ml/1 tbsp of the oil. Cook for 12 minutes, turning once.

2 Transfer the meat to a warm plate. Pour off the excess fat from the pan and return to the heat. Allow the sediment to sizzle and brown, add the rum or sherry and loosen the sediment with a flat wooden spoon. Pour the pan contents over the meat, cover and keep warm. Wipe the pan clean.

3 Heat the remaining vegetable oil in the pan and soften the onion over a steady heat.

4 Cover the peaches with boiling water to loosen the skins, then peel and slice the fruit and discard the stones (pits).

5 Add the peaches and peppercorns to the onion and coat for 3–4 minutes, until they begin to soften.

6 Add the remaining chicken stock and simmer briefly. Return the pork and meat juices to the pan, sharpen with vinegar, and season to taste. Serve with the rice.

Chicken Roll

The roll can be prepared and cooked the day before and will freeze well too. Remove from the refrigerator about an hour before serving.

Serves 8

INGREDIENTS
1 chicken, about 2kg/4lb

FOR THE STUFFING
1 medium onion, finely chopped
50g/2oz/4 tbsp melted butter
350g/12oz lean minced (ground)
   pork
115g/4oz streaky (fatty) bacon,
   chopped
15ml/1 tbsp chopped fresh parsley
10ml/2 tsp chopped fresh thyme
115g/4oz/2 cups fresh white
   breadcrumbs
30ml/2 tbsp sherry
1 large (US extra large) egg, beaten
25g/1oz/¼ cup shelled pistachio
   nuts
25g/1oz/¼ cup pitted black olives
   (about 12)
salt and ground black pepper

black olives

breadcrumbs

pork

thyme

onion

bacon   butter

1 To make the stuffing, cook the chopped onion gently in 25g/1oz/2 tbsp butter until soft. Turn into a bowl and cool. Add the remaining ingredients, except the butter, mix thoroughly and season with salt and ground black pepper.

4 To stuff the chicken, lay it flat, skin side down, and level the flesh as much as possible. Shape the stuffing down the centre of the chicken and fold the sides over the stuffing.

5 Sew the flesh neatly together using a needle and dark thread. Tie with fine string into a roll.

2 To bone the chicken, use a small, sharp knife to remove the wing tips (pinions). Lay the chicken on its breast and cut a line down the backbone.

3 Cut the flesh away from the carcass, scraping the bones clean. Carefully cut through the sinew around the leg and wing joints and scrape down the bones to free them. Remove the carcass, taking care not to cut through the skin along the breast bone.

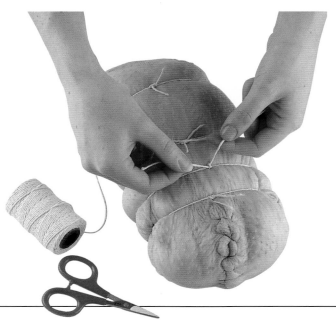

COOK'S TIPS

Thaw the chicken roll from frozen for 12 hours in the refrigerator, and leave to stand at cool room temperature for an hour before serving.

Use dark thread for sewing, as it is much easier to see so that you can remove it once the roll is cooked.

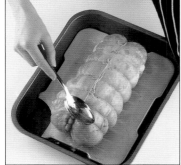

6 Preheat the oven to 180°C/350°F/ Gas 4. Place the roll, with the join underneath, on a roasting rack in a roasting pan and brush generously with the remaining butter. Bake uncovered for about 1¼ hours or until cooked. Baste the chicken often with the juices in the roasting pan. Leave to cool completely before removing the string and thread. Wrap in foil and chill until ready for serving or freezing.

Swiss Cheese, Chicken and Tongue Salad with Apple and Celery

The rich sweet flavours of this salad marry well with the tart peppery nature of watercress. A minted lemon dressing combines to freshen the overall effect. Serve with warm new potatoes.

Serves 4

INGREDIENTS
2 free-range chicken breasts, skin and bone removed
½ chicken stock (bouillon) cube
225g/8oz sliced ox (beef) tongue or ham, 6mm/¼in thick
225g/8oz Gruyère cheese
1 lollo rosso lettuce
1 butterhead or Batavian endive lettuce
1 bunch watercress
2 green-skinned apples, cored and sliced
3 celery sticks, sliced
60ml/4 tbsp sesame seeds, toasted
salt, ground black pepper and nutmeg

FOR THE DRESSING
75ml/5 tbsp groundnut (peanut) or sunflower oil
5ml/1 tsp sesame oil
45ml/3 tbsp lemon juice
10ml/2 tsp chopped fresh mint
3 drops Tabasco sauce

1 Place the chicken breasts in a pan, cover with 300ml/10fl oz water, add the ½ stock cube and bring to the boil. Put the lid on the pan and simmer for 15 minutes. Drain, reserving the stock for another use, then cool the chicken under cold running water.

2 To make the dressing, measure the two oils, lemon juice, mint and Tabasco sauce into a screw-top jar and shake. Cut the chicken, tongue and cheese into fine strips. Moisten with a little dressing and set aside.

3 Wash and spin the salad leaves, combine with the apple and celery, and dress. Distribute between 4 large plates. Pile the chicken, tongue and cheese in the centre, sprinkle with toasted sesame seeds, season with salt, black pepper and freshly grated nutmeg and serve.

lollo rosso lettuce

ox tongue

celery

watercress

butterhead lettuce

chicken breast

Gruyère cheese

Chicken Liver, Bacon and Tomato Salad

Warm salads are especially welcome during the late summer months when the evenings are growing cooler. Try this rich salad with sweet spinach and bitter leaves of frisée lettuce.

Serves 4

INGREDIENTS
225g/8oz young spinach, stems removed
1 frisée lettuce
105ml/7 tbsp groundnut (peanut) or sunflower oil
175g/6oz rindless unsmoked bacon, chopped
75g/3oz day-old bread, crusts removed, cut into short fingers
450g/1lb chicken livers
125g/4oz cherry tomatoes
salt and ground black pepper

chicken livers

spinach

bacon

cherry tomatoes

bread

2 To make the croûtons, fry the bread in the bacon-flavoured oil, tossing until crisp and golden. Drain on kitchen paper.

3 Heat the remaining 45ml/3 tbsp of oil in the frying pan, add the chicken livers and fry briskly for 2–3 minutes. Turn the livers out over the salad leaves, and add the bacon, croûtons and tomatoes. Season, toss and serve.

1 Wash and spin the salad leaves. Place in a salad bowl. Heat 60ml/4 tbsp of the oil in a large frying pan. Add the bacon and cook for 3–4 minutes or until crisp and brown. Remove the bacon with a slotted spoon and drain on a piece of kitchen paper.

Grilled Chicken Salad with Lavender and Sweet Herbs

Lavender may seem like an odd salad ingredient, but its delightful scent has a natural affinity with sweet garlic, orange and other wild herbs. A serving of polenta makes this salad both filling and delicious.

Serves 4

INGREDIENTS
4 boneless chicken breasts
850ml/1½ pints/3¾ cups light
   chicken stock
175g/6oz/1 cup fine polenta
   or cornmeal
50g/2oz butter
450g/1lb young spinach
175g/6oz lamb's lettuce
8 fresh lavender sprigs
8 small tomatoes, halved
salt and ground black pepper

FOR THE LAVENDER MARINADE
6 fresh lavender flowers
10ml/2 tsp finely grated orange zest
2 garlic cloves, crushed
10ml/2 tsp clear honey
pinch of salt
30ml/2 tbsp olive oil, French or
   Italian
10ml/2 tsp chopped fresh thyme
10ml/2 tsp chopped fresh marjoram

1 To make the marinade, strip the lavender flowers from the stems and combine with the orange zest, garlic, honey and salt. Add the olive oil and herbs. Slash the chicken deeply, spread the mixture over the chicken and leave to marinate in a cool place for at least 20 minutes.

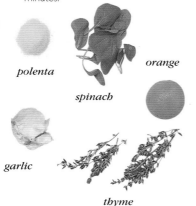

polenta

orange

spinach

garlic

lavender   *chicken breasts*

thyme

2 To make the polenta, bring the chicken stock to the boil in a heavy pan. Add the polenta in a steady stream, stirring all the time until thick: this will take 2–3 minutes. Turn the cooked polenta out on to a 2.5cm/1in-deep buttered tray and allow to cool.

3 Heat the grill (broiler) to a moderate temperature. (If using a barbecue, let the embers settle to a steady glow.) Grill (broil) the chicken for about 15 minutes, turning once.

4 Cut the polenta into 2.5cm/1in cubes with a wet knife. Heat the butter in a large frying pan and fry the polenta until golden.

COOK'S TIP

Lavender marinade is a delicious flavouring for salt-water fish as well as chicken. Try it over grilled cod, haddock, halibut, sea bass and bream or porgy.

5 Wash the salad leaves and spin dry, then divide between 4 large plates. Slice each chicken breast and lay over the salad. Place the polenta among the salad, decorate with sprigs of lavender and tomatoes, season and serve.

Tagine of Chicken

Based on a traditional Moroccan dish. The chicken and couscous can be cooked the day before and reheated for serving.

Serves 8

INGREDIENTS
8 chicken legs (thighs and drumsticks)
30ml/2 tbsp olive oil
1 medium onion, finely chopped
2 garlic cloves, crushed
5ml/1 tsp ground turmeric
2.5ml/½ tsp ground ginger
2.5ml/½ tsp ground cinnamon
450ml/¾ pint/1⅞ cups chicken
    stock
150g/5oz/1¼ cups pitted green
    olives
1 lemon, sliced
salt and ground black pepper
fresh coriander (cilantro) sprigs,
    to garnish

FOR THE VEGETABLE COUSCOUS
600ml/1 pint/2½ cups chicken stock
450g/1lb couscous
4 courgettes (zucchini),
    thickly sliced
2 carrots, thickly sliced
2 small turnips, peeled and cubed
45ml/3 tbsp olive oil
450g/15oz can chickpeas, drained

ginger
cinnamon
turmeric
green olives
couscous
onion
turnip
coriander
lemon
carrot
garlic
chickpeas
courgette
chicken stock
olive oil
chicken

1 Preheat the oven to 180°C/350°F/ Gas 4. Cut the chicken legs into two through the joint.

2 Heat the oil in a large flameproof casserole and, working in batches, brown the chicken on both sides. Remove and keep warm.

3 Add the onion and crushed garlic to the flameproof casserole and cook gently until tender. Add the spices and cook for 1 minute. Pour over the stock, bring to the boil, and return the chicken. Cover and bake for 45 minutes until tender.

4 Transfer the chicken to a bowl, cover and keep warm. Remove any fat from the cooking liquid and boil to reduce by one-third. Meanwhile, blanch the olives and lemon slices in a pan of boiling water for 2 minutes until the lemon skin is tender. Drain and add to the cooking liquid, adjusting the seasoning to taste.

5 To cook the couscous, bring the stock to the boil in a large pan and sprinkle in the couscous slowly, stirring all the time. Remove from the heat, cover and leave to stand for 5 minutes.

COOK'S TIP

The couscous can be reheated with 30ml/2 tbsp olive oil in a steamer over a pan of boiling water, stirring occasionally. If you wish to cook the chicken in advance, undercook it by 15 minutes and reheat in the oven for 20–30 minutes.

6 Meanwhile, cook the vegetables in boiling water, drain and put them into a large bowl. Add the couscous and oil and season. Stir the grains to fluff them up, add the chickpeas and finally the chopped coriander. Spoon on to a large serving plate, cover with the chicken pieces, and spoon over the liquid. Garnish with fresh coriander sprigs.

Chicken Liver Kebabs

These may be barbecued outdoors and served with salads and baked potatoes or grilled indoors and served with rice and broccoli.

Serves 4

INGREDIENTS

115g/4oz rindless streaky (fatty)
    bacon rashers (strips)
350g/12oz chicken livers
12 large (no need to pre-soak)
    pitted prunes
12 cherry tomatoes
8 button (white) mushrooms
30ml/2 tbsp olive oil

prunes

olive oil

tomatoes

mushrooms

bacon

chicken livers

1 Cut each rasher of bacon into two pieces, wrap a piece around each chicken liver and secure in position with wooden cocktail sticks (toothpicks).

2 Wrap the stoned prunes around the cherry tomatoes.

3 Thread the livers on to metal skewers with the tomatoes and prunes. Brush with oil. Cover the tomatoes and prunes with a strip of foil to protect them while grilling (broiling) or barbecuing. Cook for 5 minutes on each side.

4 Remove the cocktail sticks and serve the kebabs immediately.

Citrus Kebabs

Serve on a bed of lettuce leaves and garnish with fresh mint and citrus slices.

Serves 4

INGREDIENTS
4 chicken breasts, skinned and boned
fresh mint sprigs, to garnish
orange, lemon or lime slices, to
  garnish (optional)

FOR THE MARINADE
finely grated rind and juice of
  ½ orange
finely grated rind and juice of ½ small
  lemon or lime
30ml/2 tbsp olive oil
30ml/2 tbsp clear honey
30ml/2 tbsp chopped fresh mint
1.25ml/¼ tsp ground cumin
salt and ground black pepper

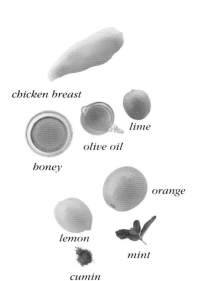

chicken breast

lime

olive oil

honey

orange

lemon

mint

cumin

1 Cut the chicken into cubes of approximately 2.5cm/1in.

2 Mix the marinade ingredients together, add the chicken cubes and leave to marinate for at least 2 hours.

3 Thread the chicken pieces on to skewers and grill (broil) or barbecue over low coals for 15 minutes, basting with the marinade and turning frequently. Serve garnished with extra mint and citrus slices, if you wish.

Kotopitta

This is based on a Greek chicken pie. Serve hot or cold with a typical Greek salad made from tomatoes, cucumber, onions and feta cheese.

Serves 4

INGREDIENTS
275g/10oz filo pastry
30ml/2 tbsp olive oil
75g/3oz/½ cup chopped toasted
   almonds
30ml/2 tbsp milk

FOR THE FILLING
15ml/1 tbsp olive oil
1 medium onion, finely chopped
1 garlic clove, crushed
450g/1lb boned and cooked chicken
50g/2oz feta cheese, crumbled
2 eggs, beaten
15ml/1 tbsp chopped fresh parsley
15ml/1 tbsp chopped fresh
   coriander (cilantro)
15ml/1 tbsp chopped fresh mint
salt and ground black pepper

chicken

olive oil

feta cheese

eggs

parsley

almonds

mint

onion

coriander

filo pastry

1 For the filling, heat the oil in a large frying pan and cook the onion gently until tender. Add the garlic clove and cook for a further 2 minutes. Transfer to a bowl.

2 Remove the skin from the chicken and chop finely. Add to the onion with the rest of the filling ingredients. Mix thoroughly and season with salt and ground black pepper.

3 Preheat the oven to 190°C/375°F/Gas 5. Have a damp dish towel ready to keep the filo pastry covered at all times. You will need to work fast, as the pastry dries out very quickly when exposed to air. Unravel the pastry and cut the whole batch into a 30cm/12in square.

4 Taking half the sheets (cover the remainder), brush one sheet with a little olive oil, lay it on a well greased 1.35 litre/2¼ pint ovenproof dish and sprinkle with a few chopped toasted almonds. Repeat with the other sheets, overlapping them alternately into the dish.

5 Spoon in the filling and cover the pie in the same way with the rest of the overlapping pastry.

6 Fold in the overlapping edges and mark a diamond pattern on the surface of the pie with a sharp knife. Brush with milk and sprinkle on any remaining almonds. Bake for 20–30 minutes or until golden brown on top.

Warm Duck Salad with Orange and Coriander

The rich gamey flavour of duck provides the foundation for this delicious salad. Serve it on cool summer evenings and enjoy the warm flavours of orange and coriander.

Serves 4

INGREDIENTS
1 small orange
2 boneless duck breasts
150ml/5fl oz/²⁄₃ cup dry white wine
5ml/1 tsp ground coriander seeds
½ tsp ground cumin or fennel seeds
30ml/2 tbsp caster (superfine)
    sugar
juice of ½ small lime or lemon
75g/3oz day-old bread, thickly sliced
45ml/3 tbsp garlic oil
½ escarole lettuce
½ frisée lettuce
30ml/2 tbsp sunflower or groundnut
    (peanut) oil
salt and cayenne pepper
4 fresh coriander (cilantro) sprigs,
    to garnish

1 Halve the orange and slice thickly. Discard any stray pips (seeds) and place the slices in a small pan. Cover with water, bring to the boil and simmer for 5 minutes to remove the bitterness. Drain and set aside.

bread

duck breast

coriander

orange

escarole lettuce

lime

frisée lettuce

2 Pierce the skin of the duck breasts diagonally with a small knife (this will help release the fat as they cook). Rub the skin with salt. Place a steel or cast-iron frying pan over a steady heat and cook the breasts for 20 minutes, turning once, until they are medium-rare. Transfer to a warm plate, cover and keep warm. Pour the duck fat into a small bowl and set aside for another use.

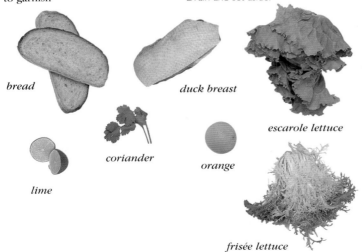

3 Heat the sediment in the frying pan until it begins to darken and caramelize. Add the wine and stir to loosen the sediment. Add the ground coriander, cumin, sugar and orange slices. Boil quickly and reduce to a coating consistency. Sharpen with lime juice and season to taste with salt and cayenne pepper. Transfer to a bowl, cover and keep warm.

4 To make the garlic croûtons, remove the crusts from the bread and discard them. Cut the bread into short fingers. Heat the garlic oil in a heavy frying pan and brown until evenly crisp. Season with salt, then turn out on to kitchen paper.

5 Wash the salad leaves and spin dry. Moisten with sunflower oil and distribute between 4 large serving plates.

6 Slice the duck breasts diagonally with a carving knife. Divide the breast meat into 4 and lift on to each salad plate. Spoon on the dressing, sprinkle with croûtons, decorate with a sprig of coriander and serve.

COOK'S TIP
Duck breast has the quality of red meat and is cooked either rare, medium or well done according to taste.

Minty Lamb Burgers with Redcurrant Chutney

These rather special burgers, with their surprise filling of creamy mozzarella cheese, take a little extra time to prepare but are well worth it.

Serves 4

500g/1¼lb minced (ground) lean lamb
1 small onion, finely chopped
30ml/2 tbsp finely chopped fresh mint
30ml/2 tbsp finely chopped fresh parsley
115g/4oz mozzarella cheese
salt and ground black pepper

FOR THE CHUTNEY
115g/4oz/1½ cups fresh or frozen redcurrants
10ml/2 tsp clear honey
5ml/1 tsp balsamic vinegar
30ml/2 tbsp finely chopped fresh mint

redcurrants

mint

minced lamb

balsamic vinegar

clear honey

mozzarella cheese   *parsley*

onion

COOK'S TIP
If time is short, or if fresh redcurrants are not available, serve the burgers with redcurrant sauce from a jar.

1 Mix together the lamb, onion, mint and parsley until evenly combined; season well with salt and pepper.

2 Divide the mixture into eight equal pieces and use your hands to press them into flat rounds.

3 Cut the mozzarella into four slices or cubes. Place them on four of the lamb rounds. Top each with another round of meat mixture.

4 Press together firmly, making four flattish burger shapes and sealing in the cheese completely.

5 Place all the ingredients for the chutney in a bowl and mash them together with a fork. Season well with salt and pepper.

6 Brush the lamb patties with oil and cook them over a moderately hot barbecue for about 15 minutes, turning once, until golden brown. Serve with the redcurrant chutney.

Grilled Mediterranean Vegetables with Marbled Yogurt Pesto

Chargrilled summer vegetables – a meal on its own, or delicious served as an accompaniment to grilled meats and fish.

Serves 4

2 small aubergines (eggplants)
2 large courgettes (zucchini)
1 red (bell) pepper
1 yellow (bell) pepper
1 fennel bulb
1 red onion
olive oil, for brushing
salt and ground black pepper

FOR THE SAUCE
150ml/¼ pint/⅔ cup Greek
    (US strained plain) yogurt
45ml/3 tbsp pesto

aubergines

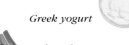
olive oil

pesto

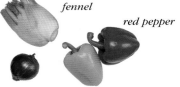
courgettes

Greek yogurt

fennel

red pepper

red onion   *yellow pepper*

COOK'S TIP
Baby vegetables make excellent candidates for grilling whole, so look out for baby aubergines (eggplants) and (bell) peppers, in particular. There's no need to salt the aubergines, if they're small.

1 Cut the aubergines into 1cm/½in thick slices. Sprinkle with salt and leave to drain for about 30 minutes. Rinse and dry well.

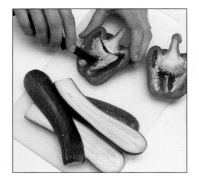

2 Cut the courgettes in half lengthways. Cut the peppers in half, remove the seeds but leave the stalk on.

3 Slice the fennel and the onion into thick wedges.

4 Stir the yogurt and pesto lightly together, to make a marbled sauce. Spoon into a serving bowl.

5 Brush the vegetables with oil and sprinkle with salt and ground black pepper. Arrange the aubergines and peppers on the hot barbecue and cook for 2–3 minutes, turning occasionally.

6 Add the courgettes, onion and fennel and cook for 4–5 minutes more, until all the vegetables are golden brown and tender. Serve with the marbled yogurt and pesto sauce.

Peppered Steaks in Beer and Garlic

Robust flavours for hearty appetites. Serve with salad and baked potatoes.

Serves 4

4 beef sirloin or rump (round)
    steaks, 2.5cm/1in thick, about
    175g/6oz each
2 garlic cloves, crushed
120ml/4fl oz/½ cup brown ale
    or stout
30ml/2 tbsp dark muscovado
    (molasses) sugar
30ml/2 tbsp Worcestershire
    sauce
15ml/1 tbsp corn oil
15ml/1 tbsp crushed black
    peppercorns

dark muscovado sugar

brown ale

beef steaks

Worcestershire sauce

garlic

corn oil

black peppercorns

COOK'S TIP
Take care when basting with
the reserved marinade, as the
alcohol will tend to flare up;
spoon or brush on just a small
amount at a time.

1 Place the steaks in a deep dish and add the garlic, ale or stout, sugar, Worcestershire sauce and oil. Turn to coat evenly in the marinade, and then leave to marinate in the refrigerator for 2–3 hours or overnight.

2 Remove the steaks from the dish and reserve the marinade. Sprinkle the peppercorns over the steaks and press them into the surface.

3 Cook the steaks on a hot barbecue, basting them occasionally during cooking, with the reserved marinade.

4 Turn the steaks once during cooking, and cook them for 3–6 minutes on each side, depending on how rare you like them.

Indonesian Pork and Peanut Satay

These delicious skewers of pork are popular street food in Indonesia. They are quick to make and eat.

Serves 4

INGREDIENTS
400g/14oz/2 cups long grain rice
450g/1lb lean pork
pinch of salt
2 limes, quartered, to garnish
115g/4oz green salad, to serve

FOR THE BASTE AND DIP
15ml/1 tbsp vegetable oil
1 small onion, chopped
1 garlic clove, crushed
2.5ml/½ tsp hot chilli sauce
15ml/1 tbsp sugar
30ml/2 tbsp soy sauce
30ml/2 tbsp lemon or lime juice
75ml/5 tbsp water
2.5ml/½ tsp anchovy essence
   (paste) (optional)
60ml/4 tbsp smooth peanut butter

lemon

lime

rice

peanut butter

pork

garlic

chilli sauce

1 Place the rice in a large pan with 900ml/1½ pints/3¾ cups of boiling salted water, stir and simmer uncovered for 15 minutes, until the liquid has been absorbed. Switch off the heat, cover and stand for 5 minutes. Slice the pork into thin strips, then thread zig-zag fashion on to 16 bamboo skewers.

2 Heat the vegetable oil in a pan. Add the onion and cook over a gentle heat to soften without colouring for about 3–4 minutes. Add the next 6 ingredients and the anchovy essence, if using. Simmer briefly, then stir in the peanut butter.

3 Preheat a moderate grill, spoon a third of the sauce over the pork and cook for 6–8 minutes, turning once. Spread the rice out on to a serving dish, place the pork satay on top and serve with the dipping sauce. Garnish with quartered limes and serve with a green salad.

VARIATION
Indonesian satay can also be prepared with lean beef, chicken or prawns (shrimp).

Grilled Chicken with Pica de Gallo Salsa

This dish originates from Mexico. Its hot, fruity flavours form the essence of Tex-Mex Cooking.

COOK'S TIP
To capture the spirit of Tex-Mex food, cook the chicken over a barbecue and eat shaded from the hot summer sun.

Serves 4

INGREDIENTS
4 chicken breast portions
pinch of celery salt and cayenne
    pepper combined
30ml/2 tbsp vegetable oil
corn chips, to serve

FOR THE SALSA
275g/10oz watermelon
175g/6oz cantaloupe melon
1 small red onion
1–2 green chillies
30ml/2 tbsp lime juice
60ml/4 tbsp chopped fresh coriander
    (cilantro)
pinch of salt

green chillies

chicken breasts

red onion

lime

coriander

cantaloupe melon

watermelon

1 Preheat a moderate grill (broiler). Slash the chicken breast portions deeply to speed up the cooking time.

2 Season the chicken with celery salt and cayenne, brush with oil and grill (broil) for about 15 minutes.

3 To make the salsa, remove the rind and as many seeds as you can from the melons. Finely dice the flesh and put it into a bowl.

4 Finely chop the onion, split the chillies (discarding the seeds, which contain most of the heat) and chop. Take care not to touch sensitive skin areas when handling cut chillies. Mix with the melon.

5 Add the lime juice and chopped coriander, and season with a pinch of salt. Turn the salsa into a small bowl.

6 Arrange the grilled chicken on a plate and serve with the salsa and a handful of corn chips.

Mexican Beef Burgers

Nothing beats the flavour and quality of a home-made burger. This version is from Mexico and is seasoned with cumin and fresh coriander.

Makes 4

INGREDIENTS
4 corn cobs
50g/2oz/1 cup stale white
    breadcrumbs
90ml/6 tbsp milk
1 small onion, finely chopped
5ml/1 tsp ground cumin
2.5ml/½ tsp cayenne pepper
2.5ml/½ tsp celery salt
45ml/3 tbsp chopped fresh
    coriander (cilantro)
900g/2lb lean minced (ground)
    beef
4 sesame buns
60ml/4 tbsp mayonnaise
4 tomato slices
½ iceberg lettuce or other leaves
    such as frisée or Webb's
salt and ground black pepper
1 large packet corn chips, to serve

iceberg lettuce

minced beef

onion

tomatoes

sesame buns

white bread

1 Bring a large pan of water to the boil, add a good pinch of salt and cook the corn cobs for 15 minutes.

2 Combine the breadcrumbs, milk, onion, cumin, cayenne, celery salt and fresh coriander in a large bowl.

3 Add the beef and mix by hand until evenly blended.

4 Divide the mixture into four portions and flatten between sheets of clear film (plastic wrap).

5 Preheat a moderate grill (broiler) and cook for 10 minutes for medium burgers or 15 minutes for well-done burgers, turning once during the cooking time.

6 Split and toast the buns, spread with mayonnaise and sandwich the burgers with the tomato slices, lettuce leaves and seasoning. Serve with corn chips and the corn cobs.

COOK'S TIP
If planning ahead, freeze the burgers between sheets of baking parchment or clear film (plastic wrap). Covered, they will keep well for up to twelve weeks. Thaw before cooking.

Minted Egg and Fennel Tabbouleh with Toasted Hazelnuts

Tabbouleh, a Middle-Eastern dish of steamed bulgur wheat, is suited to warm-weather picnics.

Serves 4

INGREDIENTS
250g/9oz/1¼ cups bulgur wheat
2 eggs
1 fennel bulb
1 bunch spring onions (scallions),
    chopped
25g/1oz sun-dried tomatoes, sliced
45ml/3 tbsp chopped fresh parsley
30ml/2 tbsp chopped fresh mint
75g/3oz black olives
60ml/4 tbsp olive oil, preferably
    Greek or Spanish
30ml/2 tbsp garlic oil
30ml/2 tbsp lemon juice
1 cos or romaine lettuce
50g/2oz chopped hazelnuts, toasted
salt and ground black pepper
1 medium open-textured loaf or
    4 pitta breads, warmed, to serve

1 Cover the bulgur wheat with boiling water and leave to soak for 15 minutes. Transfer to a metal sieve (strainer), position over a pan of boiling water, cover and steam for 10 minutes. Spread out on a metal tray and leave to cool.

2 Hard-boil the eggs for 12 minutes. Cool under running water, shell and quarter. Halve and finely slice the fennel. Boil in salted water for 6 minutes, drain and cool under running water. Combine the eggs, fennel, spring onions, sun-dried tomatoes, parsley, mint and olives with the bulgur wheat. Dress with olive oil, garlic oil and lemon juice. Season well.

3 Wash the lettuce leaves and spin dry. Line an attractive salad bowl or plate with the leaves, pile in the tabbouleh and sprinkle with toasted hazelnuts. Serve with a basket of warmed bread.

COOK'S TIP
A popular way to eat tabbouleh is to shovel it into pockets of pitta bread. In Middle Eastern countries guests are invited to wrap tabbouleh in lettuce.

cos lettuce

hazelnuts

fennel

mint

eggs

parsley

sun-dried tomatoes

spring onions

olives

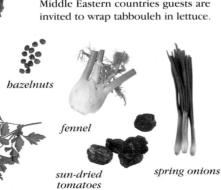

Chinese Chicken Wings

These are best eaten with fingers as a first course, so make sure you provide finger bowls and plenty of paper napkins.

Serves 4

INGREDIENTS
12 chicken wings
3 garlic cloves, crushed
4cm/1½in piece fresh root
   ginger, grated
juice of 1 large lemon
45ml/3 tbsp soy sauce
45ml/3 tbsp clear honey
2.5ml/½ tsp chilli powder
150ml/¼ pint/⅔ cup chicken stock
salt and ground black pepper
lemon wedges, to garnish

garlic

lemon

chicken wings

soy sauce

honey   chilli powder

ginger

1 Remove the wing tips (pinions) and use to make the stock. Cut the wings into two joints.

2 Mix the remaining ingredients together and coat the chicken pieces in the mixture completely. Cover with clear film (plastic wrap) and place in the refrigerator to marinate overnight.

3 Preheat the oven to 220°C/425°F/Gas 7. Remove the wings from the marinade and arrange in a single layer in a roasting pan. Bake for 20–25 minutes, basting at least twice with the marinade during cooking.

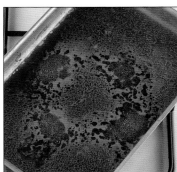

4 Place the wings on a serving plate. Add the stock to the marinade in the roasting pan, and bring to the boil. Cook to a syrupy consistency and spoon a little over the wings. Serve garnished with lemon wedges.

Koftas

A fun way to serve spicy minced lamb.
These tasty kebabs are packed with the flavours
of the Mediterranean.

Serves 4

INGREDIENTS
450g/1lb/4 cups minced (ground)
    lamb
75g/3oz/1½ cups fresh wholemeal
    (whole-wheat) breadcrumbs
1 onion, grated
5ml/1 tsp ground cumin
2 garlic cloves, crushed
1 egg, beaten
60ml/2fl oz/¼ cup lamb stock
salt and ground black pepper

breadcrumbs

egg

garlic

cumin

minced lamb

onion

1 Place the minced lamb in a bowl and mash with a fork to form a paste.

2 Add the breadcrumbs and onion.

3 Stir in the cumin and garlic. Season well to taste.

4 Stir in the egg and stock with a fork. Using your hands bind the mixture together until smooth.

5 Shape into "sausages" with lightly floured hands.

COOK'S TIP
Soak the wooden skewers in cold water for 30 minutes before using to prevent them from burning.

6 Thread on to wooden kebab skewers and grill (broil) under a medium heat for 30 minutes, turning occasionally. Serve with a crisp green salad.

Chicken Pasties

These individual chicken and Stilton pies are wrapped in a crisp shortcrust pastry and shaped into pasties. They can be served hot or cold.

Makes 4

INGREDIENTS
350g/12oz/3 cups self-raising (self-rising) flour
2.5ml/½ tsp salt
75g/3oz/6 tbsp lard or white cooking fat
75g/3oz/6 tbsp butter
60–75ml/4–5 tbsp cold water
beaten egg, to glaze

FOR THE FILLING
450g/1lb boned and skinned chicken thighs
25g/1oz/¼ cup chopped walnuts
25g/1oz spring onions (scallions), sliced
50g/2oz/½ cup Stilton cheese, crumbled
25g/1oz celery, finely chopped
2.5ml/½ tsp dried thyme
salt and ground black pepper

butter

spring onions

celery

stilton

thyme

flour

chicken thighs

1 Preheat the oven to 200°C/400°F/ Gas 6. Mix the flour and salt in a bowl. Rub in the lard and butter with your fingers until the mixture resembles fine breadcrumbs. Using a knife to cut and stir, mix in the cold water to form a stiff, pliable dough.

2 Turn out on to a board and knead lightly until smooth. Divide into four equal pieces and roll out each piece to a thickness of 5mm/¼in, keeping a good round shape. Cut into a 20cm/8in circle, using a plate as a guide.

3 Remove any fat from the chicken thighs and cut into small cubes. Mix with the walnuts, spring onions, Stilton, celery, thyme and seasoning and divide between the four pastry circles.

4 Brush the edge of the pastry with beaten egg and fold over, pinching and crimping the edges together well. Place on a greased baking tray and bake in the preheated oven for about 45 minutes or until golden brown.

Tandoori Chicken

A popular party dish. The chicken is marinated the night before so all you have to do on the day is to cook it in a very hot oven and serve with wedges of lemon and green salad.

Serves 4

INGREDIENTS
1 chicken, about 1.75kg/3½lb,
    cut into 8 pieces
juice of 1 large lemon
150ml/½ pint/⅔ cup low-fat natural
    (plain) yogurt
3 garlic cloves, crushed
30ml/2 tbsp olive oil
5ml/1 tsp ground turmeric
10ml/2 tsp ground paprika
5ml/1 tsp grated fresh root ginger
    or 2.5ml/½ tsp ground
10ml/2 tsp garam masala
5ml/1 tsp salt
a few drops of red food colouring
    (optional)

lemon
olive oil
garlic
ginger
yogurt
garam masala
chicken
paprika
turmeric

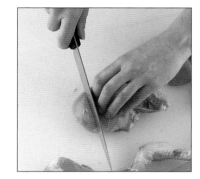

1 Skin the chicken pieces and cut two slits in each piece.

2 Arrange in a single layer in a dish and pour over the lemon juice.

3 Mix together the remaining ingredients and pour the sauce over the chicken pieces, turning them to coat thoroughly. Cover with clear film (plastic wrap) and chill overnight.

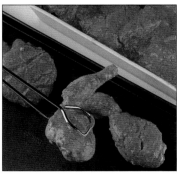

4 Preheat the oven to 220°C/425°F/ Gas 7. Remove the chicken from the marinade and arrange in a single layer in a shallow baking tray. Bake for 15 minutes, turn over, and cook for a further 15 minutes or until tender.

Mexico Barbecued Salmon

If you intend to barbecue the salmon, make sure the barbecue is heated up thoroughly before you start to cook. It should take the same cooking time as conventional grilling.

Serves 4

INGREDIENTS
1 small red onion
1 garlic clove
6 plum tomatoes
25g/1oz/2 tbsp butter
45ml/3 tbsp tomato ketchup
30ml/2 tbsp Dijon mustard
30ml/2 tbsp dark brown sugar
15ml/1 tbsp runny honey
5ml/1 tsp cayenne pepper
15ml/1 tbsp ancho chilli powder
15ml/1 tbsp ground paprika
15ml/1 tbsp Worcestershire sauce
4 salmon fillets, about
    175g/6oz each

cayenne pepper

Dijon mustard

dark brown sugar

plum tomatoes

salmon fillet

red onion

tomato ketchup

1 Finely chop the red onion and finely dice the garlic.

2 Dice the tomatoes.

3 Melt the butter in a large, heavy pan and gently cook the onion and garlic until translucent.

4 Add the tomatoes and simmer for 15 minutes.

5 Add the remaining ingredients except the salmon and simmer for a further 20 minutes. Process the mixture in a food processor fitted with a metal blade and leave to cool.

6 Brush the salmon with the sauce and chill for at least 2 hours. Barbecue or grill for about 2–3 minutes either side, brushing on the sauce when necessary.

Stilton Burger

Slightly more up-market than the traditional burger, this tasty recipe contains a delicious surprise. The lightly melted Stilton cheese encased in a crunchy burger is absolutely delicious.

Serves 4

INGREDIENTS
450g/1lb/4 cups minced
   (ground) beef
1 onion, finely chopped
1 celery stick, chopped
5ml/1 tsp dried mixed herbs
5ml/1 tsp prepared mustard
50g/2oz/½ cup crumbled Stilton
   cheese
4 burger buns
salt and ground black pepper

celery

minced beef

Stilton cheese

onion

dried herbs

burger buns   *mustard*

1 Place the minced beef in a bowl together with the onion and celery. Season well.

2 Stir in the herbs and mustard, bringing them together to form a firm mixture.

3 Divide the mixture into eight equal portions. Place four on a chopping board and flatten each one slightly.

4 Place the crumbled cheese in the centre of each.

5 Flatten the remaining mixture and place on top. Mould the mixture together, encasing the crumbled cheese, and shape into four burgers.

6 Grill (broil) under a medium heat for 10 minutes, turning once, until cooked through. Split the burger buns and place a burger inside each. Serve with salad and mustard pickle.

Salami Hero

This is a huge affair, filled with as much as you can cram into a roll. This American speciality varies regionally, and can contain tuna, egg, cheese, coleslaw, salads, meats or salamis according to your taste, or whatever is available.

Makes 2

INGREDIENTS
2 long crusty rolls
25g/1oz/2 tbsp butter, softened
a few leaves lollo rosso lettuce
    or radicchio
75g/3oz coleslaw
75g/3oz Italian salami, sliced
1 tomato, sliced
30ml/2 tbsp mayonnaise

lollo rosso lettuce

rolls

tomato   *Italian salami*

mayonnaise

coleslaw

1 Cut the rolls horizontally three-quarters of the way through, open out sufficiently to take the filling and butter both cut sides.

2 Arrange lettuce or radicchio leaves on the base, then add a spoonful of coleslaw.

3 Fold the salami slices in half and arrange over the top. Cover with a little more lettuce, tomato slices and a little mayonnaise. Serve with a napkin!

Classic BLT

This delicious American sandwich is made with crispy fried bacon, lettuce and tomato. Choose the bread you prefer and toast it if you like.

Makes 2

INGREDIENTS
4 slices Granary (whole-wheat) bread
15g/½oz/1 tbsp butter, softened
a few crisp lettuce leaves, such as cos, romaine or iceberg
1 large tomato, sliced
8 rashers (strips) streaky (fatty) bacon
30ml/2 tbsp mayonnaise

Granary bread

tomato

lettuce

bacon

1 Spread 2 of the slices of bread with butter. Lay the lettuce over the bread and cover with sliced tomato.

2 Grill (broil) the bacon rashers until they begin to crisp, then arrange them over the sliced tomato.

3 Spread the 2 remaining slices of bread with mayonnaise. Lay over the bacon, press the sandwich together gently and cut in half.

Pan Bagna

This literally means 'bathed bread' and is basically a Salade Niçoise stuffed into a baguette or roll. The olive oil dressing soaks into the bread when it is left for an hour or so with a weight on top of it.

Makes 4

INGREDIENTS
1 large baguette
150ml/5fl oz/²/₃ cup French Dressing
1 small onion, thinly sliced
3 tomatoes, sliced
1 small green or red (bell) pepper,
    seeded and sliced
50g/2oz can anchovy fillets, drained
90g/3½oz can tuna, drained
50g/2oz black olives, halved
    and pitted

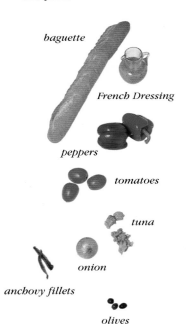

baguette

French Dressing

peppers

tomatoes

tuna

onion

anchovy fillets

olives

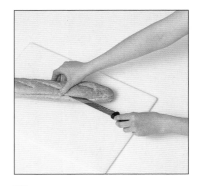

1 Split the baguette horizontally along one side without cutting all the way through the crust.

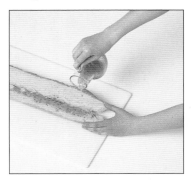

2 Open the bread out so that it lies flat and sprinkle the French Dressing evenly over the top.

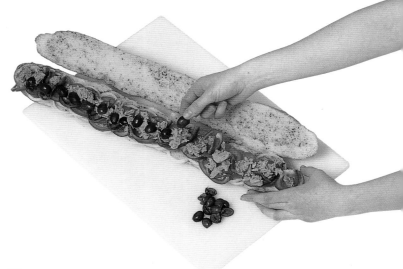

3 Arrange the onion, tomatoes, green or red pepper, anchovies, tuna and olives on one side of the bread. Close the 2 halves, pressing firmly together.

4 Wrap in clear film (plastic wrap), lay a board on top, put a weight on it and leave for about 1 hour: as well as allowing the dressing to soak into the bread, this makes it easier to eat.

5 Cut the loaf diagonally into 4 equal portions.

FRENCH DRESSING

Olive oil is a must for this dressing; it imparts a rich, fruity flavour, especially if you use that lovely green extra virgin olive oil. Make a large quantity at a time and store it in a wine bottle, ready for instant use.

Makes about 450ml/ ³/₄ pint/scant 2 cups

350ml/12fl oz/1¹/₂ cups extra virgin olive oil
90ml/6 tbsp red wine vinegar
15ml/1 tbsp Moutarde de Meaux or other French mustard
1 garlic clove, crushed
5ml/1 tsp clear honey
salt and ground black pepper

Pour the olive oil into a measuring jug and make up to 450ml/³/₄ pint/scant 2 cups with the vinegar. Add the remaining ingredients, then, using a funnel pour into a wine bottle. Put in the cork firmly, give the mixture a thorough shake and store.

Farmer's Brunch

A new and tasty twist to a traditional, wholesome sandwich. Use very fresh crusty white bread and top the cheese with a home-made Peach Relish, which goes particularly well with Red Leicester cheese.

Makes 2

INGREDIENTS
4 slices crusty white bread
25g/1oz/2 tbsp butter, softened
100g/4oz Red Leicester or
    Wensleydale cheese, sliced
45ml/3 tbsp Peach Relish
spring onions (scallions) or
    pickled onions, and tomato
    wedges, to serve

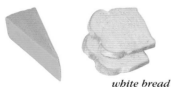

white bread

Red Leicester

tomato

spring onion

Peach Relish

1 Butter the bread.

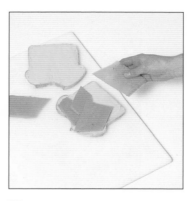

2 Cover 2 slices with cheese.

3 Spread Peach Relish over the remaining 2 slices and place them over the cheese.

4 Cut in half and serve with spring onions or pickled onions, and tomato wedges.

PEACH RELISH

This delicious and very quick relish can be eaten immediately. It will keep for up to 1 month in the refrigerator.

Makes about 700ml/ 25fl oz/3 cups

60ml/4 tbsp wine vinegar
60ml/4 tbsp soft light brown sugar
5ml/1 tsp finely chopped chilli
5ml/1 tsp finely chopped fresh
    root ginger
5 peaches, stoned (pitted)
    and chopped

1 yellow (bell) pepper, seeded
    and chopped
1 small onion, chopped

Put the vinegar and sugar in a pan with the chilli and ginger and heat gently until the sugar has dissolved.
    Add the remaining ingredients and bring to the boil, stirring constantly.
    Cover and cook gently for 15 minutes. Remove the lid and cook for a further 10–15 minutes until tender and the liquid is slightly reduced. Pour into warm, clean jars and cover.

Cannelloni

This Italian dish has fast become popular, offering many variations to the original recipe. This version introduces a variety of vegetables which are topped with a traditional cheese sauce.

Serves 4

INGREDIENTS
15ml/1 tbsp oil
175g/6oz/1½ cups minced (ground) beef
2 garlic cloves, crushed
25g/1oz/2 tbsp plain (all-purpose) flour
120ml/4fl oz/½ cup beef stock
1 small carrot, finely chopped
1 small yellow courgette (zucchini), chopped
8 cannelloni tubes
115g/4oz spinach
salt and ground black pepper

FOR THE SAUCE
25g/1oz/2 tbsp butter
25g/1oz/2 tbsp plain (all-purpose) flour
250ml/8fl oz/1 cup milk
50g/2oz/½ cup freshly grated Parmesan cheese

minced beef　　*spinach*

garlic

cannelloni　*carrot*　　*courgette*　　*butter*　*Parmesan cheese*

1 Preheat the oven to 180°C/350°F/ Gas 4. For the filling, heat the oil in a large pan. Add the minced beef and garlic. Cook for 5 minutes.

2 Add the flour and cook for a further 1 minute. Slowly stir in the stock and bring to the boil.

3 Add the carrot and courgette, season well and cook for 10 minutes.

4 Spoon the beef mixture into the cannelloni tubes and place in an ovenproof dish.

5 Blanch the spinach in boiling water for 3 minutes. Drain well and place on top of the cannelloni tubes.

6 For the sauce, melt the butter in a pan. Add the flour and cook for 1 minute. Pour in the milk, add the grated cheese and season well. Bring to the boil, stirring all the time, until thickened. Pour over the cannelloni and spinach and cook for 30 minutes in the preheated oven. Serve with tomatoes and a crisp green salad.

Pasta Bows with Smoked Salmon and Dill

In Italy, pasta cooked with smoked salmon is becoming very fashionable. This is a quick and luxurious sauce.

Serves 4

INGREDIENTS
6 spring onions (scallions), sliced
50g/2oz/4 tbsp butter
90ml/6 tbsp dry white wine or
    vermouth
450ml/15fl oz/2 cups double
    (heavy) cream
freshly grated nutmeg
225g/8oz smoked salmon
30ml/2 tbsp chopped fresh dill or
    15ml/1 tbsp dried
freshly squeezed lemon juice
450g/1lb/4 cups pasta bows (farfalle)
salt and ground black pepper

pasta bows

lemon

spring onions

smoked salmon

nutmeg

dill

1 Slice the spring onions finely. Melt the butter in a pan and fry the spring onions for about 1 minute until soft.

2 Add the wine and boil hard to reduce to about 30ml/2tbsp. Stir in the cream and add salt, pepper and nutmeg to taste. Bring to the boil and simmer for 2–3 minutes until slightly thickened.

3 Cut the smoked salmon into 2.5cm/1in squares and stir into the sauce with the dill. Taste and add a little lemon juice. Keep warm.

4 Cook the pasta in plenty of boiling salted water according to the manufacturer's instructions. Drain well. Toss the pasta with the sauce and serve immediately.

Stir-fried Vegetables with Pasta

This is a colourful Chinese-style dish, easily prepared using pasta instead of Chinese noodles.

Serves 4

INGREDIENTS

1 medium carrot
175g/6oz small courgettes (zucchini)
175g/6oz runner or other green beans
175g/6oz baby corn
450g/1lb ribbon pasta, such as tagliatelle
30ml/2 tbsp corn oil, plus extra for tossing the pasta
1cm/½in piece fresh root ginger, peeled and finely chopped
2 garlic cloves, finely chopped
90ml/6 tbsp yellow bean sauce
6 spring onions (scallions), sliced into 2.5cm/1in lengths
30ml/2 tbsp dry sherry
5ml/1 tsp sesame seeds
salt and ground black pepper

green beans

baby sweetcorn

tagliatelle

root ginger

spring onions

courgettes

garlic

1 Slice the carrot and courgettes diagonally into chunks. Slice the beans diagonally. Cut the baby corn diagonally in half.

2 Cook the pasta in plenty of boiling salted water according to the manufacturer's instructions, drain, then rinse under hot water. Toss in a little oil.

3 Heat 30ml/2 tbsp oil until smoking in a wok or frying pan and add the ginger and garlic. Stir-fry for 30 seconds, then add the carrots, beans and courgettes.

4 Stir-fry for 3–4 minutes, then stir in the yellow bean sauce. Stir-fry for 2 minutes, add the spring onions, sherry and pasta and stir-fry for a further minute until piping hot. Sprinkle with sesame seeds and serve immediately.

Penne with Aubergine and Mint Pesto

This splendid variation on the classic Italian pesto uses fresh mint rather than basil for a different flavour.

Serves 4

INGREDIENTS
2 large aubergines (eggplants)
salt
450g/1lb penne
50g/2oz walnut halves

FOR THE PESTO
25g/1oz fresh mint
15g/½oz flat leaf parsley
40g/1½oz walnuts
40g/1½oz Parmesan cheese, finely
  grated
2 garlic cloves
90ml/6 tbsp olive oil
salt and ground black pepper

penne

garlic

walnuts

aubergine

olive oil

parsley

mint

Parmesan

1 Cut the aubergines lengthways into 1cm/½in slices.

2 Cut the slices again crossways to give short strips.

3 Layer the strips in a colander with salt and leave to stand for 30 minutes over a plate to catch any juices. Rinse well in cool water and drain.

4 Place all the pesto ingredients except the oil in a blender or food processor, blend until smooth, then gradually add the oil in a thin stream until the mixture amalgamates. Season to taste.

5 Cook the penne following the instructions on the side of the packet for about 8 minutes or until nearly cooked. Add the aubergine and cook for a further 3 minutes.

6 Drain well and mix in the mint pesto and walnut halves. Serve immediately.

Margherita Pizza

(Tomato, Basil and Mozzarella)
This classic pizza is simple to prepare. The sweet flavour of sun-ripe tomatoes works wonderfully with the basil and mozzarella.

Serves 2–3

INGREDIENTS
1 pizza base, about 25–30cm/10–12in
   diameter
30ml/2 tbsp olive oil
1 quantity Tomato Sauce
150g/5oz mozzarella
2 ripe tomatoes, thinly sliced
6–8 fresh basil leaves
30ml/2 tbsp freshly grated Parmesan
   cheese
ground black pepper

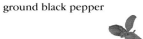

basil

mozzarella

Parmesan

olive oil

Tomato Sauce

tomatoes

1 Preheat the oven to 220°C/425°F/Gas 7. Brush the pizza base with 15ml/1 tbsp of the oil and then spread over the Tomato Sauce.

2 Cut the mozzarella into thin slices.

3 Arrange the sliced mozzarella and tomatoes on top of the pizza base.

4 Roughly tear the basil leaves, add and sprinkle with the Parmesan. Drizzle over the remaining oil and season with black pepper. Bake for 15–20 minutes until crisp and golden. Serve immediately.

Marinara Pizza

(Tomato and Garlic)

The combination of garlic, good-quality olive oil and oregano gives this pizza an unmistakably Italian flavour.

Serves 2–3

INGREDIENTS
60ml/4 tbsp olive oil
675g/1½lb plum tomatoes, peeled, seeded and chopped
1 pizza base, about 25–30cm/10–12in in diameter
4 garlic cloves, cut into slivers
15ml/1 tbsp chopped fresh oregano
salt and ground black pepper

olive oil

oregano

plum tomatoes

garlic

1 Preheat the oven to 220°C/425°F/Gas 7. Heat 30ml/2 tbsp of the oil in a pan. Add the tomatoes and cook, stirring frequently, for about 5 minutes until soft.

2 Place the tomatoes in a sieve (strainer) and leave them to drain for about 5 minutes.

3 Transfer the tomatoes to a food processor or blender and purée until smooth.

4 Brush the pizza base with half the remaining oil. Spoon over the tomatoes and sprinkle with garlic and oregano. Drizzle over the remaining oil and season. Bake for 15–20 minutes until crisp and golden. Serve immediately.

American Hot Pizza

This popular pizza is spiced with green chillies and pepperoni.

Serves 2–3

INGREDIENTS
1 pizza base, about 25–30cm/10–12in
  diameter
15ml/1 tbsp olive oil
115g/4oz can peeled and chopped
  green chillies in brine, drained
1 quantity Tomato Sauce (see Tip)
75g/3oz sliced pepperoni
6 pitted black olives
15ml/1 tbsp chopped fresh oregano
115g/4oz mozzarella cheese, grated
oregano leaves, to garnish

mozzarella

oregano

pepperoni

Tomato Sauce

olive oil

green chillies

black olives

1 Preheat the oven to 220°C/425°F/ Gas 7. Brush the pizza base with the oil.

2 Stir the chillies into the sauce, and spread over the base.

3 Arrange the pepperoni on top.

4 Halve the olives lengthways and sprinkle over, with the oregano.

5 Sprinkle over the grated mozzarella and bake for 15–20 minutes, until the pizza is crisp and golden.

COOK'S TIP

To make Tomato Sauce to cover a 25–30cm/10–12in round pizza base: heat 15ml/1 tbsp olive oil in a pan and add 1 finely chopped onion and 1 crushed garlic clove. Fry gently for 5 minutes then add a 400g/14oz can chopped tomatoes, 15ml/1 tbsp tomato purée (paste), 15ml/1 tbsp chopped fresh mixed herbs, a pinch each of sugar, salt and black pepper. Simmer for about 20 minutes or until the sauce is thick. Leave to cool completely before use.

6 Garnish with oregano leaves and serve immediately.

Capellini with Rocket, Mangetout and Pine Nuts

A light but filling pasta dish with the added pepperiness of fresh rocket.

Serves 4

INGREDIENTS

250g/9oz capellini or angel-hair pasta
225g/8oz mangetout (snow peas)
175g/6oz rocket (arugula)
50g/2oz/¼ cup pine nuts, roasted
30ml/2 tbsp Parmesan cheese, finely grated (optional)
30ml/2 tbsp olive oil (optional)

rocket

Parmesan

pine nuts

capellini

mange-tout

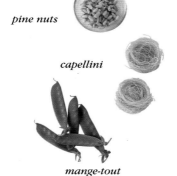

COOK'S TIP
Olive oil and Parmesan are optional as they obviously raise the fat content.

1 Cook the capellini or angel-hair pasta following the instructions on the side of the packet until *al dente*.

2 Meanwhile, carefully trim the mangetout.

3 As soon as the pasta is cooked, drop in the rocket and mangetout. Drain immediately.

4 Toss the pasta with the roasted pine nuts, and the Parmesan and olive oil if using. Serve immediately.

Pasta Bows with Fennel and Walnut Sauce

A scrumptious blend of walnuts and crisp steamed fennel.

Serves 4

INGREDIENTS
75g/3oz/½ cup walnuts, roughly
    chopped
1 garlic clove
25g/1oz fresh flat leaf parsley, picked
    from the stalks
115g/4oz/½ cup ricotta cheese
450g/1lb pasta bows
450g/1lb fennel bulbs
chopped walnuts, to garnish

garlic

pasta bows

ricotta

fennel

parsley

walnut halves

chopped walnuts

1 Place the chopped walnuts, garlic and parsley in a food processor. Pulse until roughly chopped. Transfer to a bowl and stir in the ricotta.

2 Cook the pasta following the instructions on the side of the packet until *al dente*. Drain well.

3 Slice the fennel thinly and steam for 4–5 minutes until just tender but still crisp.

4 Return the pasta to the pan and add the walnut mixture and the fennel. Toss well and sprinkle with the chopped walnuts. Serve immediately.

123

Sun-dried Tomato Bread

This savoury bread tastes delicious on its own, but it also makes exceptional sandwiches.

Makes 1 loaf

INGREDIENTS
375g/13oz/3¼ cups strong white
    bread flour
5ml/1 tsp salt
10ml/2 tsp easy-blend (rapid-rise)
    dried yeast
50g/2oz (drained weight) sun-dried
    tomatoes in oil, chopped
175ml/6fl oz/¾ cup lukewarm water
75ml/5 tbsp lukewarm olive oil, plus
    extra for brushing
plain (all-purpose) flour, for dusting

water

strong white bread flour

olive oil

easy-blend yeast

sun-dried tomatoes

salt

1 Sift the flour and salt into a large mixing bowl.

2 Stir in the yeast and sun-dried tomatoes.

3 Make a well in the centre of the dry ingredients. Pour in the water and oil, and mix until the ingredients come together and form a soft dough.

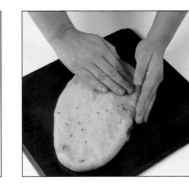

4 Turn the dough on to a lightly floured surface and knead for about 10 minutes.

5 Shape into an oblong loaf, without making the top too smooth, and place on a greased baking sheet. Brush the top with oil, cover with clear film (plastic wrap), then leave to rise in a warm place for about 1 hour.

6 Meanwhile, preheat the oven to 220°C/425°F/Gas 7. Remove the clear film, then sprinkle the top of the loaf lightly with flour. Bake for 30–40 minutes until the loaf sounds hollow when tapped on the bottom. Serve warm.

Rosemary and Sea Salt Focaccia

The delicious Italian bread is here given added flavour with fragrant rosemary, coarse sea salt and crisp red onion.

Makes 1 loaf

INGREDIENTS
350g/12oz/3 cups plain
(all-purpose) flour
2.5ml/½ tsp salt
10ml/2 tsp easy-blend (rapid-rise)
dried yeast
about 250ml/8fl oz/1 cup lukewarm
water
45ml/3 tbsp olive oil
1 small red onion
leaves from 1 large rosemary sprig
5ml/1 tsp coarse sea salt

coarse sea salt

water

olive oil

plain flour

easy-blend yeast

red onion

rosemary

1 Sift the flour and salt into a large mixing bowl. Stir in the yeast, then make a well in the centre of the dry ingredients. Pour in the water and 30ml/2 tbsp of the oil. Mix well, adding a little more water if the mixture seems dry.

2 Turn the dough on to a lightly floured surface and knead for about 10 minutes until smooth and elastic.

3 Place the dough in a greased bowl, cover and leave in a warm place for about 1 hour until doubled in size. Knock back (punch down) and knead the dough for 2–3 minutes.

4 Meanwhile, preheat the oven to 220°C/425°F/Gas 7. Roll out the dough to a large circle, about 1cm/½in thick, and transfer to a greased baking sheet. Brush with the remaining oil.

5 Halve the onion and slice into thin wedges. Sprinkle over the dough, with the rosemary and sea salt, pressing it in lightly.

6 Using a finger make deep indentations in the dough. Cover the surface with greased clear film (plastic wrap), then leave to rise in a warm place for 30 minutes. Remove the clear film and bake for 25– 30 minutes until golden. Serve warm.

Ham and Pineapple French Bread Pizza

French bread makes a great pizza base. For a really speedy recipe use ready-prepared pizza topping instead of the Tomato Sauce.

Serves 4

INGREDIENTS
2 small baguettes
1 quantity Tomato Sauce
75g/3oz sliced cooked ham
4 rings canned pineapple, drained well and chopped
½ small green (bell) pepper, seeded and cut into thin strips
75g/3oz mature (sharp) Cheddar cheese
salt and ground black pepper

green pepper

mature Cheddar

pineapple

cooked ham

baguette

Tomato Sauce

1 Preheat the oven to 200°C/400°F/ Gas 6. Cut the baguettes in half lengthways and toast the cut sides until crisp and golden.

2 Spread the Tomato Sauce over the toasted baguettes.

3 Cut the ham into strips and arrange on the baguettes with the pineapple and pepper. Season.

4 Grate the Cheddar and sprinkle on top. Bake or grill (broil) for 15–20 minutes, until crisp and golden.

Prosciutto, Roasted Peppers and Mozzarella Ciabatta Pizzas

Succulent roasted peppers, salty prosciutto and creamy mozzarella – the delicious flavours of these easy pizzas are hard to beat.

Serves 2

INGREDIENTS
½ loaf ciabatta bread
1 red and 1 yellow (bell) pepper, roasted and peeled
4 slices prosciutto, cut into thick strips
75g/3oz mozzarella cheese
ground black pepper
tiny basil leaves, to garnish

ciabatta

basil

mozzarella

prosciutto

red and yellow peppers

1 Cut the ciabatta bread into four thick slices and toast both sides until golden.

2 Cut the roasted peppers into thick strips and arrange on the toasted bread with the Parma ham.

3 Thinly slice the cheese and arrange on top. Grind over plenty of pepper. Place under a hot grill (broiler) for 2–3 minutes until the cheese is bubbling.

4 Arrange the basil leaves on top and serve immediately.

Spaghetti Olio e Aglio

This is a classic recipe from Rome. A quick and filling dish, originally the food of the poor involving nothing more than pasta, garlic and olive oil, it is now fast becoming fashionable.

Serves 4

INGREDIENTS
2 garlic cloves
30ml/2 tbsp fresh parsley
100ml/4fl oz/½ cup olive oil
450g/1lb spaghetti
salt and ground black pepper

spaghetti

olive oil

parsley

garlic

1 Finely chop the garlic.

2 Chop the parsley roughly.

3 Heat the olive oil in a medium pan and add the garlic and a pinch of salt. Cook gently, stirring all the time, until golden. Take care not to let the garlic become too brown, or it will taste bitter.

4 Meanwhile cook the spaghetti in plenty of boiling salted water according to the manufacturer's instructions until *al dente*. Drain well.

5 Toss with the warm – not sizzling – garlic and oil and add plenty of black pepper and the parsley. Serve immediately.

Fiorentina Pizza

Spinach is the star ingredient of this pizza. A grating of nutmeg to heighten its flavour gives this pizza its unique character.

Serves 2–3

INGREDIENTS
175g/6oz fresh spinach
45ml/3 tbsp olive oil
1 small red onion, thinly sliced
1 pizza base, about 25–30cm/10–12in
   in diameter
1 quantity Tomato Sauce
freshly grated nutmeg
150g/5oz mozzarella
1 small (US medium) egg
25g/1oz Gruyère, grated

Gruyère

mozzarella

Tomato Sauce

spinach

red onion

nutmeg

egg

1 Preheat the oven to 220°C/425°F/Gas 7. Remove the stalks from the spinach and wash the leaves in plenty of cold water. Drain well and pat dry with kitchen paper.

2 Heat 15ml/1 tbsp of the oil and fry the onion until soft. Add the spinach and continue to fry until just wilted. Drain off any excess liquid.

3 Brush the pizza base with half the remaining oil. Spread over the Tomato Sauce, then top with the spinach mixture. Grate over some nutmeg.

4 Thinly slice the mozzarella and arrange over the spinach. Drizzle over the remaining oil. Bake for 10 minutes, then remove from the oven.

5 Make a small well in the centre and drop the egg into the hole.

6 Sprinkle over the Gruyère and return to the oven for a further 5–10 minutes until crisp and golden. Serve immediately.

Mini Focaccia with Pine Nuts

Pine nuts add little bites of nutty texture to these mini focaccias.

Makes 4 mini loaves

INGREDIENTS
350g/12oz/3 cups plain
    (all-purpose) flour
2.5ml/½ tsp salt
10ml/2 tsp easy-blend (rapid-rise)
    dried yeast
about 250ml/8fl oz/1 cup lukewarm
    water
45ml/3 tbsp olive oil
45–60ml/3–4 tbsp pine nuts
10ml/2 tsp coarse sea salt

water

sea salt

olive oil

plain flour

easy-blend yeast

pine nuts

1 Sift the flour and salt into a large mixing bowl. Stir in the yeast, then make a well in the centre of the dry ingredients. Pour in the water and 30ml/2 tbsp of the oil. Mix well, adding more water if the mixture seems dry. Turn on to a lightly floured surface and knead for about 10 minutes until smooth and elastic. Place the dough in a greased bowl, cover and leave in a warm place for about 1 hour until doubled in size. Knock back (punch down) and knead for 2–3 minutes.

2 Divide the dough into four pieces.

3 Using your hands pat out each piece on greased baking sheets to a 10 × 7.5cm/ 4 × 3in oblong, rounded at the ends.

4 Sprinkle over the pine nuts and gently press them into the surface. Sprinkle with salt and brush with the remaining oil. Cover with greased clear film (plastic wrap) and leave to rise for about 30 minutes. Meanwhile, preheat the oven to 220°C/425°F/Gas 7. Remove the clear film and bake the focaccias for 15–20 minutes until golden. Serve warm.

Walnut Bread

The nutty flavour of this wonderfully textured bread is excellent. Try it toasted and topped with melting goat's cheese for a mouth-watering snack.

Makes 2 loaves

INGREDIENTS
600g/1lb 5oz/4 cups strong white bread flour
10ml/2 tsp salt
10ml/2 tsp easy-blend (rapid-rise) dried yeast
150g/5oz/1¼ cups chopped walnuts
60ml/4 tbsp chopped fresh parsley
400ml/14fl oz/1⅔ cups lukewarm water
60ml/4 tbsp olive oil

strong white flour

olive oil

easy-blend yeast

parsley

walnuts

salt

1 Sift the flour and salt into a large mixing bowl. Stir in the yeast, walnuts and parsley.

2 Make a well in the centre of the dry ingredients. Pour in the water and oil and mix to a soft dough. Turn the dough on to a lightly floured surface and knead for about 10 minutes until smooth and elastic. Place in a greased bowl, cover and leave in a warm place for about 1 hour until doubled in size.

3 Knock back (punch down) and knead the dough for 2–3 minutes. Divide in half and shape each piece into a thick roll about 18–20cm/7–8in long. Place on greased baking sheets, cover with clear film (plastic wrap) and leave to rise for about 30 minutes.

4 Meanwhile, preheat the oven to 220°C/425°F/Gas 7. Remove the clear film, then lightly slash the top of each loaf. Bake for 10 minutes, then reduce the oven temperature to 180°C/350°F/Gas 4 and bake for a further 25–30 minutes until the loaves sound hollow when tapped. Serve warm.

Quattro Stagioni Pizza

(Four Seasons)
This traditional pizza is divided into quarters, each with a different topping, to depict the four seasons of the year.

Serves 2–4

INGREDIENTS
45ml/3 tbsp olive oil
50g/2oz button (white) mushrooms, sliced
1 pizza base, about 25–30cm/10–12in in diameter
1 quantity Tomato Sauce
50g/2oz prosciutto
6 pitted black olives, chopped
4 bottled artichoke hearts in oil, drained
3 canned anchovy fillets, drained
50g/2oz mozzarella cheese, thinly sliced
8 fresh basil leaves, shredded
ground black pepper

artichoke hearts

mozzarella

olive oil

Tomato Sauce

prosciutto

basil

black olives

button mushrooms

anchovy fillets

1 Preheat the oven to 220°C/425°F/Gas 7. Heat 15ml/1 tbsp of the oil in a frying pan and fry the mushrooms until all the juices have evaporated. Leave to cool.

2 Brush the pizza base with half the remaining oil. Spread over the Tomato Sauce and mark into four equal sections with a knife.

3 Arrange the mushrooms over one section of the pizza.

4 Cut the prosciutto into strips and arrange with the olives on another section of the pizza.

5 Thinly slice the artichoke hearts and arrange over a third section. Halve the anchovies lengthways and arrange with the mozzarella over the fourth section.

6 Sprinkle over the basil. Drizzle over the remaining oil and season with black pepper. Bake for 15–20 minutes until crisp and golden. Serve immediately.

Pasta with Roasted Pepper and Tomato Sauce

Add other vegetables such as French beans or courgettes (zucchini) or even chickpeas to make this sauce more substantial.

Serves 4

INGREDIENTS
2 medium red (bell) peppers
2 medium yellow (bell) peppers
45ml/3 tbsp olive oil
1 medium onion, sliced
2 garlic cloves, crushed
2.5ml/½ tsp mild chilli powder
400g/14oz can chopped
    plum tomatoes
450g/1lb/4 cups dried pasta shells
    or spirals
salt and ground black pepper
freshly grated Parmesan cheese,
    to serve

peppers

pasta shells

onion

garlic

1 Preheat the oven to 200°C/400°F/ gas mark 6. Place the peppers on a baking sheet or in a roasting pan and bake for about 20 minutes or until beginning to char. Alternatively grill (broil) the peppers, turning them frequently.

2 Rub the skins off the peppers under cold water. Halve, remove the seeds and roughly chop the flesh.

3 Heat the oil in a medium pan and add the onion and garlic. Cook gently for 5 minutes, until soft and golden.

4 Stir in the chilli powder, cook for 2 minutes, then add the tomatoes and peppers. Bring to the boil and simmer for 10–15 minutes until slightly thickened and reduced. Season to taste.

5 Cook the pasta in plenty of boiling salted water according to the manufacturer's instructions. Drain well and toss with the sauce. Serve piping hot with lots of Parmesan cheese.

Soft Leeks with Parsley, Egg and Walnut Dressing

In French cooking leeks are valued for their smooth texture as well as for their flavour. Here they are served as a *salade tiède* (warm salad), with an earthy-rich sauce of parsley, egg and walnut. Serve as a side salad with grilled or poached fish and new potatoes.

Serves 4

INGREDIENTS
700g/1½lb young leeks
1 egg

FOR THE DRESSING
25g/1oz fresh parsley
30ml/2 tbsp olive oil, preferably
    French
juice of ½ lemon
50g/2oz/½ cup broken walnuts,
    toasted
5ml/1 tsp caster (superfine) sugar
salt and ground black pepper

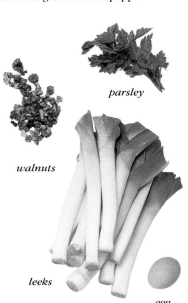

parsley

walnuts

leeks

egg

1 Bring a pan of salted water to the boil. Cut the leeks into 10cm/4in lengths and rinse well to flush out any grit or soil. Cook the leeks for 8 minutes. Drain and part-cool under running water.

2 Lower the egg into boiling water and cook for 12 minutes. Cool under running water, shell and set aside.

3 For the dressing, finely chop the parsley in a food processor.

4 Add the olive oil, lemon juice and toasted walnuts. Blend for 1–2 minutes until smooth.

5 Adjust the consistency with about 90ml/6 tbsp/⅓ cup water. Add the sugar and season to taste with salt and pepper.

6 Place the leeks on a serving plate, then spoon over the sauce. Finely grate the hard-boiled egg over the sauce. Serve at room temperature.

Goat's Cheese Salad with Buckwheat, Fresh Figs and Walnuts

The robust flavours of goat's cheese and buckwheat combine especially well with ripe figs and walnuts. The olive and nut oil dressing contains no vinegar and depends instead on the acidity of the cheese. Enjoy this dish with a gutsy red wine from the Rhône or the South of France.

Serves 4

INGREDIENTS
175g/6oz/¾ cup couscous
30ml/2 tbsp toasted buckwheat
1 egg, hard-boiled
30ml/2 tbsp chopped fresh parsley
60ml/4 tbsp olive oil, preferably Sicilian
45ml/3 tbsp walnut oil
125g/4oz rocket (arugula)
½ frisée lettuce
175g/6oz crumbly white goat's cheese
50g/2oz broken walnuts, toasted
4 ripe figs, trimmed and almost cut into four (leave the pieces joined at the base)

1 Place the couscous and buckwheat in a bowl, cover with boiling water and leave to soak for 15 minutes. Place in a sieve (strainer) if necessary to drain off any remaining water, then spread out on a metal tray and allow to cool.

rocket

goat's cheese

egg

parsley

figs

frisée lettuce

2 Shell the hard-boiled egg and pass it through a fine grater.

3 Toss the egg, parsley and couscous in a bowl. Combine the two oils and use half to moisten the couscous mixture.

4 Wash and spin the salad leaves, dress with the remaining oil and distribute between 4 large plates.

COOK'S TIP

Goats' cheeses vary in strength from the youngest, which are soft and mild, to strongly flavoured mature cheeses which have a firm and crumbly texture. Crumbly cheeses are best suited for salads.

5 Pile the couscous in the centre, crumble on the goat's cheese, sprinkle with toasted walnuts and add the figs.

Caesar Salad

There are many stories about the origin of Caesar Salad. The most convincing is that it was invented by an Italian, Caesar Cardini, who owned a restaurant in Mexico in the 1920s. Simplicity is the key to the dish's success.

Serves 4

INGREDIENTS
3 slices day-old bread, 1cm/½in thick
60ml/4 tbsp garlic oil
50g/2oz piece Parmesan cheese
1 cos or romaine lettuce
salt and ground black pepper

DRESSING
2 egg yolks, as fresh as possible
25g/1oz canned anchovy fillets, roughly chopped
½ tsp French mustard
125ml/4fl oz/½ cup olive oil, preferably Italian
15ml/1 tbsp white wine vinegar

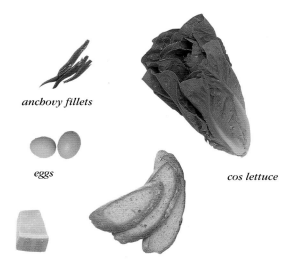

anchovy fillets

eggs

cos lettuce

Parmesan cheese   *bread*

1 To make the dressing, combine the egg yolks, anchovies, mustard, oil and vinegar in a screw-top jar and shake well.

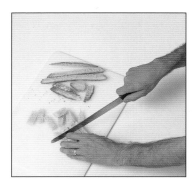

2 Remove the crusts from the bread with a serrated knife and cut into 2.5cm/1in fingers.

3 Heat the garlic oil in a large frying pan, add the pieces of bread and fry until golden. Remove from the pan, sprinkle with salt and leave to drain on absorbent kitchen paper.

4 Cut thin shavings from the Parmesan cheese with a vegetable peeler.

5 Wash the salad leaves and spin dry. Smother with the dressing, and sprinkle with garlic croûtons and Parmesan cheese. Season and serve.

Potato Salad with Egg and Lemon Dressing

Potato salads are a popular addition to any salad spread and are enjoyed with an assortment of cold meats and fish. This recipe draws on the contrasting flavours of egg and lemon. Chopped parsley provides a fresh finish.

Serves 4

INGREDIENTS
900g/2lb new potatoes, scrubbed
   or scraped
1 medium onion, finely chopped
1 egg, hard-boiled
300ml/10fl oz/1¼ cups mayonnaise
1 garlic clove, crushed
finely grated zest and juice of 1 lemon
60ml/4 tbsp chopped fresh parsley
salt and ground black pepper

COOK'S TIP
At certain times of the year potatoes are inclined to fall apart when boiled. This usually coincides with the end of a particular season when potatoes become starchy. Early-season varieties are therefore best for making salads.

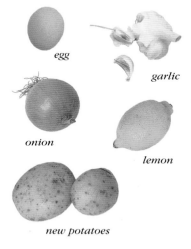

egg

garlic

onion

lemon

new potatoes

1 Bring the potatoes to the boil in a pan of salted water. Simmer for 20 minutes. Drain and allow to cool. Cut the potatoes into large dice, season well and combine with the onion.

2 Shell the hard-boiled egg and grate into a mixing bowl, then add the mayonnaise. Combine the garlic and lemon zest and juice in a small bowl and stir into the mayonnaise.

3 Fold in the chopped parsley, mix thoroughly into the potatoes and serve.

Tomato and Feta Cheese Salad

Sweet sun-ripened tomatoes are rarely more delicious than when served with feta cheese and olive oil. This salad, popular in Greece and Turkey, is enjoyed as a light meal with pieces of crispy bread.

Serves 4

INGREDIENTS
900g/2lb tomatoes
200g/7oz feta cheese
125ml/4fl oz/½ cup olive oil, preferably Greek
12 black olives
4 fresh basil sprigs
ground black pepper

COOK'S TIP
Feta cheese has a strong flavour and can be salty. The least salty variety is imported from Greece and Turkey, and is available from specialist delicatessens.

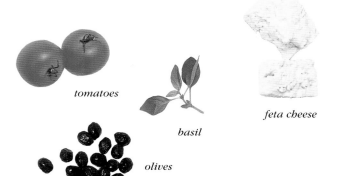

tomatoes

basil

olives

feta cheese

2 Slice the tomatoes thickly and arrange in a shallow dish.

3 Crumble the cheese over the tomatoes, sprinkle with olive oil, then strew with olives and fresh basil. Season with freshly ground black pepper and serve at room temperature.

1 Remove the tough cores from the tomatoes with a small knife.

Spicy Vegetable Fritters with Thai Salsa

The Thai salsa goes just as well with plain stir-fried salmon strips or stir-fried beef as it does with these vegetable fritters.

Serves 2–4

INGREDIENTS
10ml/2 tsp cumin seeds
10ml/2 tsp coriander seeds
450g/1lb courgettes (zucchini)
115g/4oz/1 cup gram flour
2.5ml/½ tsp bicarbonate of soda
    (baking soda)
125ml/4fl oz/½ cup groundnut
    (peanut) oil
salt and ground black pepper
fresh mint sprigs, to garnish

FOR THE THAI SALSA
½ cucumber, diced
3 spring onions (scallions),
    chopped
6 radishes, cubed
30ml/2 tbsp fresh mint, chopped
2.5cm/1in piece fresh root ginger,
    peeled and grated
45ml/3 tbsp lime juice
30ml/2 tbsp caster (superfine)
    sugar
3 garlic cloves, crushed

cucumber

mint

ginger

radishes

courgette

1 Heat a wok, then dry-fry the cumin and coriander seeds until they begin to pop. Cool them, then grind well, using a pestle and mortar.

2 Cut the courgettes into 7.5cm/3in sticks. Place in a bowl.

3 Blend the flour, bicarbonate of soda, spices, and salt and black pepper in a food processor. Add 125ml/4fl oz warm water with 15ml/1 tbsp groundnut oil, and blend again.

4 Coat the courgettes in the batter, then leave to stand for 10 minutes.

5 To make the Thai salsa, mix all the ingredients together in a bowl.

6 Heat the wok, then add the remaining oil. When the oil is hot, stir-fry the courgettes in batches. Drain well on kitchen paper, then serve hot with the salsa, garnished with fresh mint sprigs.

Tzatziki

Tzatziki is a Greek cucumber salad dressed with yogurt, mint and garlic. It is typically served as an accompaniment to grilled lamb and chicken, but is also good with salmon and trout.

Serves 4

INGREDIENTS
1 cucumber
5ml/1 tsp salt
45ml/3 tbsp finely chopped fresh
  mint, plus a few sprigs, to garnish
1 garlic clove, crushed
5ml/1 tsp caster (superfine) sugar
200ml/7fl oz Greek (US strained
  plain) yogurt
paprika, to garnish (optional)

mint

cucumber

1 Peel the cucumber. Reserve a little to use as a garnish if you wish and cut the rest in half lengthways. Remove the seeds with a teaspoon and discard. Slice the cucumber thinly and combine with the salt in a bowl. Leave for approximately 15–20 minutes. Salt will soften the cucumber and draw out any bitter juices.

2 Thoroughly combine the mint, garlic, sugar and yogurt in a bowl.

3 Rinse the cucumber in a sieve (strainer) under cold running water to flush away the salt. Drain well and combine with the yogurt. Decorate with cucumber and mint. Serve cold. Tzatziki is traditionally garnished with paprika.

COOK'S TIP

If preparing Tzatziki in a hurry, leave out the method for salting cucumber at the end of step 1. The cucumber will have a more crunchy texture, and will be slightly less sweet.

Green Bean Salad with Egg Topping

When green beans are fresh and plentiful, serve them lightly cooked as a salad starter topped with butter-fried breadcrumbs, egg and parsley.

Serves 4

INGREDIENTS
700g/1½lb green beans, trimmed
salt
30ml/2 tbsp garlic oil
30ml/2 tbsp butter
50g/2oz/1 cup fresh white
  breadcrumbs
60ml/4 tbsp chopped fresh parsley
1 egg, hard-boiled and shelled

2 Heat the butter in a large frying pan, add the breadcrumbs and fry until golden. Remove from the heat, add the parsley, then grate in the hard-boiled egg

3 Place the beans in a shallow serving dish and spoon on the breadcrumb topping. Serve at room temperature.

1 Bring a large pan of salted water to the boil. Add the beans and cook for 6 minutes. Drain well, toss in garlic oil and allow to cool.

parsley

egg

green beans

COOK'S TIP
Few cooks need reminding how to boil an egg, but many are faced with the problem of a dark ring around the yolk when cooked. This is caused by boiling for longer than the optimum period of 12 minutes. Allow boiled eggs to cool in water for easy peeling.

Fruit and Fibre Salad

Fresh, fast and filling, this salad makes a great starter, supper or snack.

Serves 4–6

INGREDIENTS
225g/8oz red or white cabbage
   or a mixture
3 medium carrots
1 pear
1 red-skinned eating apple
200g/7oz can green flageolet
   or cannellini beans, drained
50g/2oz/¼ cup chopped dates

FOR THE DRESSING
2.5ml/½ tsp dry English (hot)
   mustard
10ml/2 tsp clear honey
30ml/2 tbsp orange juice
5ml/1 tsp white wine vinegar
2.5ml/½ tsp paprika
salt and ground black pepper

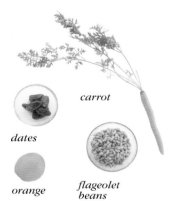

carrot

dates

orange

flageolet beans

cabbage   *pear*   *apple*

1 Shred the cabbage very finely, discarding any tough stalks.

2 Cut the carrots into very thin strips, about 5cm/2in long.

3 Quarter, core and slice the pear and apple, leaving the skin on.

4 Put the fruit and vegetables in a bowl with the beans and dates. Mix well.

5 For the dressing, blend the mustard with the honey until smooth. Add the orange juice, vinegar, paprika and seasoning and mix well.

6 Pour the dressing over the salad and toss to coat. Chill in the refrigerator for 30 minutes before serving.

Mixed Stir-fried Vegetables

Frying with Parmesan cheese in this unusual way gives a wonderful crusty coating to the vegetables and creates a truly Mediterranean flavour.

Serves 4 as an accompaniment

INGREDIENTS
1 large aubergine (eggplant), about 225g/8oz
salt, for sprinkling
175g/6oz plum tomatoes
2 red (bell) peppers
1 yellow (bell) pepper
30ml/2 tbsp olive oil
25g/1oz Parmesan cheese
30ml/2 tbsp fresh parsley, chopped
ground black pepper

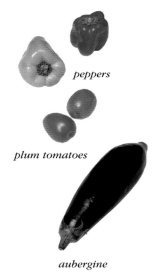

peppers

plum tomatoes

aubergine

1 Cut the aubergine into segments lengthways. Place in a colander and sprinkle with salt. Leave for 30 minutes, to allow the salt to draw out the bitter juices.

2 Rinse off the salt under cold water and pat dry on kitchen paper.

3 Cut the plum tomatoes into segments lengthways.

4 Cut the red and yellow peppers into quarters lengthways and remove the seeds.

5 Heat a wok, then add 5ml/1 tsp of the olive oil. When the oil is hot, add the Parmesan cheese and stir-fry until golden brown. Remove from the wok, allow to cool and chop into fine flakes.

6 Heat the wok, and then add the remaining oil. When the oil is hot, stir-fry the aubergine and peppers for 4–5 minutes. Stir in the tomatoes and stir-fry for a further 1 minute. Toss the vegetables in the Parmesan, parsley and black pepper and serve.

Bulgur Wheat and Mint Salad

Also known as cracked wheat, burghul or pourgouri, bulgur wheat has been partially cooked, so it requires only a short soaking before serving.

Serves 4

INGREDIENTS
250g/9oz/1⅔ cups bulgur wheat
4 tomatoes
4 small courgettes (zucchini),
  thinly sliced lengthways
4 spring onions (scallions), sliced
  on the diagonal
8 ready-to-eat dried apricots, chopped
40g/1½oz/¼ cup raisins
juice of 1 lemon
30ml/2 tbsp tomato juice
45ml/3 tbsp chopped fresh mint
1 garlic clove, crushed
salt and ground black pepper
sprig of fresh mint, to garnish

courgettes   bulgur wheat

tomatoes

spring onions   lemon

1 Put the bulgur wheat into a large bowl. Add enough cold water to come 2.5cm/1in above the level of the wheat. Leave to soak for 30 minutes, then drain well and squeeze out any excess water in a clean dish towel.

2 Meanwhile submerge the tomatoes in boiling water for 1 minute and then plunge into cold water. Slip off their skins. Halve them, remove the seeds and cores, and roughly chop the flesh.

3 Stir the chopped tomatoes, courgettes, spring onions, apricots, and raisins into the cracked wheat.

4 Put the lemon and tomato juice, mint, garlic clove and seasoning into a small bowl and whisk together with a fork. Pour over the salad and mix well. Chill in the refrigerator for at least 1 hour. Serve garnished with a sprig of mint.

Cachumbar

Cachumbar is a salad relish most commonly served with Indian curries. There are many versions – this one will leave your mouth feeling cool and fresh after a spicy meal.

Serves 4

INGREDIENTS
3 ripe tomatoes
2 spring onions, chopped
1.5ml/¼ tsp caster (superfine)
  sugar
salt
45ml/3 tbsp chopped fresh coriander
  (cilantro)

tomatoes

coriander

spring onion

COOK'S TIP
Cachumbar also makes a fine accompaniment to fresh crab, lobster and shellfish.

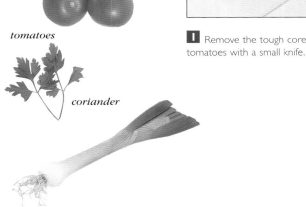

1 Remove the tough cores from the tomatoes with a small knife.

2 Halve the tomatoes, remove the seeds and dice the flesh.

3 Combine the tomatoes with the spring onions, sugar, salt and chopped coriander. Serve at room temperature.

Russian Salad

Russian salad became fashionable in the hotel dining rooms of the 1920s and 1930s. Originally it consisted of lightly cooked vegetables, egg, shellfish and mayonnaise. Today we find it diced in plastic pots in supermarkets. This version recalls better days and plays on the theme of the Fabergé egg.

Serves 4

INGREDIENTS
125g/4oz large button (white)
    mushrooms
125ml/4fl oz/½ cup mayonnaise
15ml/1 tbsp lemon juice
350g/12oz cooked peeled
    prawns (shrimp)
1 large gherkin, chopped, or
    30ml/2 tbsp capers
125g/4oz broad (fava) beans
125g/4oz small new potatoes,
    scrubbed or scraped
125g/4oz young carrots, trimmed
    and peeled
125g/4oz baby corn
125g/4oz baby turnips, trimmed
15ml/1 tbsp olive oil, preferably
    French or Italian
4 eggs, hard-boiled and shelled
25g/1oz canned anchovy fillets, cut
    into fine strips
salt, ground black pepper
    and paprika

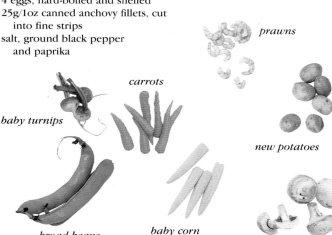

prawns

carrots

baby turnips

new potatoes

broad beans

baby corn

mushrooms

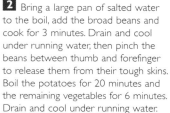

1 Slice the mushrooms thinly, then cut into matchsticks. Combine the mayonnaise and lemon juice. Fold half of the mayonnaise into the mushrooms and prawns, add the chopped gherkin, then season to taste.

2 Bring a large pan of salted water to the boil, add the broad beans and cook for 3 minutes. Drain and cool under running water, then pinch the beans between thumb and forefinger to release them from their tough skins. Boil the potatoes for 20 minutes and the remaining vegetables for 6 minutes. Drain and cool under running water.

3 Moisten the vegetables with oil and divide between 4 shallow bowls. Spoon on the dressed prawns and place a hard-boiled egg in the centre. Decorate the egg with strips of anchovy and sprinkle with paprika.

Marinated Cucumber Salad

Sprinkling the cucumber with salt draws out some of the water and makes them crisper.

Serves 4–6

INGREDIENTS
2 medium cucumbers
15ml/1 tbsp salt
90g/3½oz/½ cup granulated sugar
175ml/6fl oz/¾ cup dry
   (hard) cider
15ml/1 tbsp cider vinegar
45ml/3 tbsp chopped fresh dill
ground black pepper

cider

dill

sugar

vinegar

cucumber

1 Slice the cucumbers thinly and place them in a colander, sprinkling salt between each layer. Put the colander over a bowl and leave to drain for 1 hour.

2 Thoroughly rinse the cucumber under cold running water to remove excess salt, then pat dry on absorbent kitchen paper.

3 Gently heat the sugar, cider and vinegar in a pan, until the sugar has dissolved. Remove from the heat and leave to cool. Put the cucumber slices in a bowl, pour over the cider mixture and leave to marinate for 2 hours.

4 Drain the cucumber and sprinkle with the dill and pepper to taste. Mix well and transfer to a serving dish. Chill in the refrigerator until ready to serve.

Spinach and Potato Galette

Creamy layers of potato, spinach and herbs make a delicious supper dish.

Serves 6

INGREDIENTS
900g/2lb large potatoes
450g/1lb fresh spinach
2 eggs
400g/14oz/1¾ cup low-fat
    cream cheese
15ml/1 tbsp wholegrain mustard
50g/2oz chopped fresh herbs
    (such as chives, parsley, chervil
    or sorrel)
salt and ground black pepper

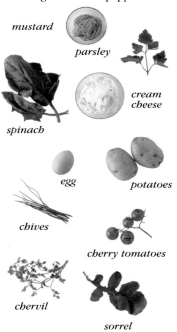

mustard

parsley

spinach

cream cheese

egg

potatoes

chives

cherry tomatoes

chervil

sorrel

1 Preheat the oven to 180°C/350°F/Gas 4. Line a deep 23cm/9in cake tin (pan) with baking parchment. Place the potatoes in a large pan and cover with cold water. Bring to the boil and cook for 10 minutes. Drain well and allow to cool slightly before slicing thinly.

2 Wash the spinach and place in a large pan with only the water that is clinging to the leaves. Cover and cook, stirring once, until the spinach has just wilted. Drain well in a sieve (strainer) and squeeze out the excess moisture. Chop finely.

3 Beat the eggs with the cream cheese and mustard then stir in the chopped spinach and fresh herbs.

4 Place a layer of the sliced potatoes in the lined tin, arranging them in concentric circles. Top with a spoonful of the cream cheese mixture and spread out. Continue layering, seasoning with salt and pepper as you go, until all the potatoes and the cream cheese mixture are used up.

5 Cover the tin with a piece of foil and place in a roasting pan.

6 Fill the roasting pan with enough boiling water to come halfway up the sides, and cook in the oven for 45–50 minutes. Turn out on to a plate and serve hot or cold.

COOK'S TIP

Choose firm potatoes for this dish such as Cara, Desirée or Estima.

Aubergine, Roast Garlic and Red Pepper Pâté

This is a simple pâté of smoky baked aubergine, sweet pink peppercorns and red peppers, with more than a hint of garlic!

Serves 4

INGREDIENTS
3 medium aubergines (eggplants)
2 red (bell) peppers
5 garlic cloves
7.5ml/1½ tsp pink peppercorns in brine, drained and crushed
30ml/2 tbsp chopped fresh coriander (cilantro)

aubergine

garlic

coriander

pink peppercorns

red pepper

1 Preheat the oven to 200°C/400°F/ Gas 6. Arrange the whole aubergines, peppers and garlic cloves on a baking sheet and place in the oven. After 10 minutes remove the garlic cloves and turn over the aubergines and peppers.

2 Peel the garlic cloves and place in the bowl of a blender.

3 After a further 20 minutes remove the blistered and charred peppers from the oven and place in a sealed plastic bag. Leave to cool.

4 After a further 10 minutes remove the aubergines from the oven. Split in half and scoop the flesh into a sieve (strainer) over a bowl. Press the flesh with a spoon to remove the bitter juices.

5 Add the mixture to the garlic in the blender and blend until smooth. Place in a large mixing bowl.

6 Peel and chop the red peppers and stir into the aubergine mixture. Mix in the peppercorns and fresh coriander and serve immediately.

Raspberry and Passion Fruit Chinchillas

Few desserts are so strikingly easy to make as this one: beaten egg whites and sugar baked in a dish, turned out and served with a handful of soft fruit.

VARIATION
If raspberries are out of season, use either fresh, bottled or canned soft berry fruit such as strawberries, blueberries or redcurrants.

Serves 4

INGREDIENTS
25g/1oz/2 tbsp butter, softened
5 egg whites
150g/5oz/²⁄₃ cup caster
    (superfine) sugar
2 passion fruit
250ml/8fl oz/1 cup ready-made
    custard from a carton or can
milk, as required
675g/1¹⁄₂lb/6 cups fresh raspberries
icing (confectioners') sugar,
    for dusting

raspberries

egg whites

passion fruit

icing sugar

1 Preheat the oven to 180°C/350°F/ Gas 4. Brush four 300ml/¹⁄₂ pint soufflé dishes with a visible layer of soft butter.

2 Whisk the egg whites in a mixing bowl until firm. (You can use an electric whisk.) Add the sugar a little at a time and whisk into a firm meringue.

3 Halve the passion fruit, take out the seeds with a spoon and fold them into the meringue.

4 Turn the meringue out into the prepared dishes, stand in a deep roasting pan which has been half-filled with boiling water, and bake for 10 minutes. The meringue will rise above the tops of the soufflé dishes.

5 Turn the chinchillas out upside-down on to a serving plate. Thin the custard with a little milk and pour around the edge of the plate.

6 Top with raspberries, dredge with icing sugar and serve warm or cold.

Red Fruit Fool

This delicious fruity dessert would be ideal for a summer lunch.

Serves 4

INGREDIENTS
450g/1lb mixed red fruit, such as
  raspberries, redcurrants and
  strawberries
10ml/2 tsp fructose
2.5ml/½ tsp arrowroot
150ml/¼ pint/⅔ cup half-fat
  whipping cream
5ml/1 tsp vanilla extract
fresh fruit, to decorate

strawberries

redcurrants

raspberries

1 Put the fruit and fructose into a large heavy pan and simmer over a low heat for 2 minutes, or until just soft.

2 Blend the arrowroot with 10ml/2 tsp cold water. Add to the fruit and simmer for a further minute, or until thickened. Cool and chill in the refrigerator for 1 hour.

3 Divide two-thirds of the fruit mixture between four individual glasses.

4 Purée the rest of the fruit and strain through a fine sieve (strainer) to remove the pips (seeds).

5 Lightly whip the cream and vanilla extract together until soft peaks form. Fold in the remaining fruit purée.

6 Spoon the fruit cream mixture between the glasses and chill for 30 minutes. Serve decorated with fresh fruit.

COOK'S TIP

Fructose is a natural fruit sugar. It is slightly sweeter than granulated sugar (sucrose), so less is needed. If you use granulated sugar instead, use 15ml/1 tbsp for this recipe.

Mandarins in Orange-flower Syrup

Mandarins, tangerines, clementines, mineolas: any of these lovely citrus fruits are suitable for this recipe.

Serves 4

INGREDIENTS
10 mandarins
15ml/1 tbsp icing (confectioners')
    sugar
10ml/2 tsp orange-flower water
15ml/1 tbsp chopped pistachio nuts

orange-flower water

pistachio nuts

mandarins

icing sugar

1 Thinly pare a little of the coloured zest from one mandarin and cut it into fine shreds for decoration. Squeeze the juice from two mandarins and reserve it.

2 Peel the remaining fruit, removing as much of the white pith as possible. Arrange the whole fruit in a wide dish.

COOK'S TIP
The mandarins look very attractive if you leave them whole, especially if there is a large quantity for a special occasion, but you may prefer to separate the segments.

3 Mix the reserved juice, sugar and orange-flower water and pour it over the fruit. Cover the dish and chill for at least 1 hour.

4 Blanch the shreds of zest in boiling water for 30 seconds. Drain, leave to cool and sprinkle them over the mandarins, with the pistachio nuts, to serve.

Redcurrant Filo Baskets

Filo pastry is light as air and makes a very elegant dessert. It's also low in fat and it needs only a fine brushing of oil before use: a light oil such as sunflower is the best choice for this recipe.

Serves 6

INGREDIENTS
3 sheets filo pastry (about
   85g/3½oz)
15ml/1 tbsp sunflower oil
175g/6oz/1½ cups redcurrants
200g/7oz/1 cup Greek (US strained
   plain) yogurt
5ml/1 tsp icing (confectioners')
   sugar

filo pastry

Greek yogurt

redcurrants

sunflower oil

icing sugar

VARIATION

Strawberries or raspberries can be substituted for redcurrants, if they are not available.

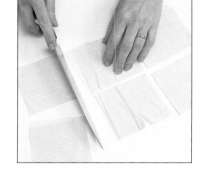

1 Preheat the oven to 200°C/400°F/ Gas 6. Cut the sheets of filo pastry into 18 squares with sides about 10cm/4in long.

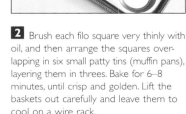

2 Brush each filo square very thinly with oil, and then arrange the squares overlapping in six small patty tins (muffin pans), layering them in threes. Bake for 6–8 minutes, until crisp and golden. Lift the baskets out carefully and leave them to cool on a wire rack.

3 Reserve a few sprigs of redcurrants on their stems for decoration and string the rest. Stir the currants into the yogurt.

4 Spoon the yogurt into the filo baskets. Decorate them with the reserved sprigs of redcurrants and sprinkle them with icing sugar to serve.

Tofu Berry 'Cheesecake'

This low-fat summery 'cheesecake' is a very light and refreshing finish to any meal. Strictly speaking, it's not a cheesecake at all, as it's based on tofu – but who would guess?

Serves 6

INGREDIENTS
50g/2oz/4 tbsp low-fat spread
30ml/2 tbsp apple juice
115g/4oz/2½ cups bran flakes or
    other high-fibre cereal

FOR THE FILLING
285g/10oz/1½ cups tofu or
    skimmed-milk soft cheese
200g/7oz/⅞ cup low-fat natural
    (plain) yogurt
15ml/1 tbsp/1 sachet powdered
    gelatine
60ml/4 tbsp apple juice

FOR THE TOPPING
175g/6oz/1¾ cups mixed summer
    soft fruit, such as strawberries,
    raspberries, redcurrants,
    blackberries etc. (or frozen "fruits
    of the forest")
30ml/2 tbsp redcurrant jelly
30ml/2 tbsp hot water

apple juice

bran flakes

summer fruit

tofu

natural yogurt

low-fat spread

1 For the base, place the low-fat spread and apple juice in a pan and heat them gently until the spread has melted. Crush the cereal and stir it into the pan.

2 Tip into a 23cm/9in loose-bottomed round flan tin (tart pan) and press down firmly. Leave to set.

3 For the filling, place the tofu or cheese and yogurt in a food processor and process until smooth. Dissolve the gelatine in the apple juice and stir the juice quickly into the tofu mixture.

4 Spread the tofu mixture over the chilled base, smoothing it evenly. Chill until the filling has set.

5 Remove the flan tin and place the 'cheesecake' on a serving plate.

6 Arrange the fruits over the top. Melt the redcurrant jelly with the hot water. Let it cool, and then spoon over the fruit to glaze.

Mango and Lime Sorbet in Lime Shells

This richly flavoured sorbet looks pretty served in the lime shells, but is also good served in scoops for a more traditional presentation.

Serves 4

INGREDIENTS
4 large limes
1 medium-size ripe mango
7.5ml/½ tbsp powdered gelatine
2 egg whites
15ml/1 tbsp granulated sugar
lime rind strips, to decorate

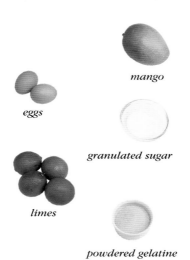

mango

eggs

granulated sugar

limes

powdered gelatine

COOK'S TIP
If you have lime juice left over from this recipe, it will freeze well for future use. Pour it into a small freezer container, seal it and freeze for up to six months. Or freeze it in useful measured amounts; pour 15ml/1 tbsp into each compartment of an ice-cube tray and freeze the tray.

1 Cut a thick slice from the top of each of the limes, and then cut a thin slice from the bottom end so that the limes will stand upright. Squeeze out the juice from the limes. Use a small knife to remove all the membrane from the centre.

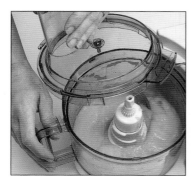

2 Halve, stone (pit), peel and chop the mango and purée the flesh in a food processor with 30ml/2 tbsp of the lime juice. Dissolve the gelatine in 45ml/3 tbsp lime juice and stir it into the mango mixture.

3 Whisk the egg whites until they hold soft peaks. Whisk in the sugar. Fold the egg white mixture quickly into the mango mixture. Spoon the sorbet into the lime shells. Any leftover sorbet that will not fit into the lime shells can be frozen in small ramekins.

4 Overwrap the filled shells with clear film (plastic wrap) and place in the freezer until the sorbet is firm. Before serving, allow the shells to stand at room temperature for about 10 minutes; decorate them with strips of lime rind.

Rhubarb and Orange Water-ice

Pretty pink rhubarb, with sweet oranges and honey – the perfect sweet ice.

Serves 4

INGREDIENTS
350g/12oz pink rhubarb
1 medium-size orange
15ml/1 tbsp clear honey
5ml/1 tsp powdered gelatine
orange slices, to decorate

clear honey

powdered gelatine

orange

rhubarb

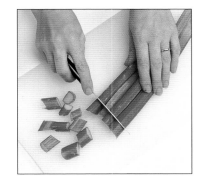

1 Trim the rhubarb and slice into 2.5cm/1in lengths. Place the rhubarb in a pan.

2 Finely grate the rind from the orange and squeeze out the juice. Add about half the orange juice and the grated rind to the rhubarb in the pan and allow to simmer until the rhubarb is just tender. Stir in the honey.

3 Heat the remaining orange juice and stir in the gelatine to dissolve. Stir it into the rhubarb. Tip the whole mixture into a rigid freezer container and freeze it until slushy, about 2 hours.

4 Remove the mixture from the freezer and beat it well to break up the ice crystals. Return the water-ice to the freezer and freeze it again until firm. Allow the water-ice to soften slightly at room temperature before serving.

COOK'S TIP

Most pink, forced rhubarb is naturally quite sweet, but if yours is not, you can add a little more honey, sugar or artificial sweetener to taste.

Summer Fruit Salad Ice Cream

What could be more cooling on a hot summer day than fresh summer fruits, lightly frozen in this irresistible ice?

Serves 6

INGREDIENTS

900g/2lb/4½ cups mixed soft summer fruit, such as raspberries, strawberries, blackcurrants, redcurrants etc.

2 eggs

225g/8oz/1 cup Greek (US strained plain) yogurt

175ml/6fl oz/¾ cup red grape juice

15ml/1 tbsp/1 sachet powdered gelatine

red grape juice

powdered gelatine

Greek yogurt

eggs

summer fruits

COOK'S TIP
Red grape juice has a good flavour and improves the colour of the ice, but if it is not available, use cranberry, apple or orange juice instead.

1 Reserve half the fruit and purée the rest in a food processor, or rub it through a sieve (strainer) to a smooth purée.

2 Separate the eggs and whisk the yolks and the yogurt into the fruit purée.

3 Heat the grape juice until almost boiling, then remove it from the heat. Sprinkle the gelatine over the grape juice and stir to dissolve the gelatine completely.

4 Whisk the dissolved gelatine mixture into the fruit purée and then pour the mixture into a freezer container. Freeze until half-frozen and slushy in consistency.

5 Whisk the egg whites until they are stiff. Quickly fold them into the half-frozen mixture.

6 Return to the freezer and freeze until almost firm. Scoop into individual dishes or glasses and add the reserved soft fruits.

Watermelon, Ginger and Grapefruit Salad

This pretty, pink combination is very light and refreshing for any summer meal.

Serves 4

INGREDIENTS
500g/1lb/2 cups diced watermelon flesh
2 ruby or pink grapefruit
2 pieces preserved stem ginger
30ml/2 tbsp stem ginger syrup

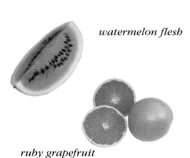

watermelon flesh

ruby grapefruit

stem ginger in syrup

COOK'S TIP
Toss the fruits gently – grapefruit segments will break up easily and the appearance of the dish will be spoiled.

1 Remove any seeds from the watermelon and cut into bite-sized chunks.

2 Using a small sharp knife, cut away all the peel and pith from the grapefruits and carefully lift out the segments, catching any juice in a bowl.

3 Finely chop the stem ginger and place in a serving bowl with the melon cubes and grapefruit segments, adding the reserved juice.

4 Spoon over the ginger syrup and toss the fruits lightly to mix evenly. Chill before serving.

Grilled Nectarines with Ricotta and Spice

This easy dessert makes a perfect end to a summer supper. Canned peach halves can also be used.

Serves 4

INGREDIENTS
4 ripe nectarines or peaches
15ml/1 tbsp light muscovado (brown) sugar
115g/4oz/½ cup ricotta cheese or fromage frais
2.5ml/½ tsp ground star anise

nectarines

light muscovado sugar

ricotta cheese

ground star anise

1 Cut the nectarines in half and remove the stones.

2 Arrange the nectarines, cut side upwards, in a wide flameproof dish or on a baking sheet.

COOK'S TIP
Star anise has a warm, rich flavour – if you can't get it, try ground cloves or mixed spice instead.

3 Stir the sugar into the ricotta or fromage frais. Using a teaspoon, spoon the mixture into the hollow of each nectarine half.

4 Sprinkle with the star anise. Place under a moderate grill (broiler) for 6–8 minutes, or until the nectarines are hot and bubbling. Serve warm.

Lemon Hearts with Strawberry Sauce

These elegant little hearts are light as air, and they are best made the day before your dinner party – which saves on last-minute panics as well!

Serves 6

INGREDIENTS
175g/6oz/¾ cup ricotta cheese
150ml/¼ pint/⅔ cup crème fraîche or sour cream
15ml/1 tbsp granulated sugar
finely grated rind of ½ lemon
30ml/2 tbsp lemon juice
15ml/1 tbsp powdered gelatine
2 egg whites

FOR THE SAUCE
225g/8oz/2 cups fresh or frozen and thawed strawberries
15ml/1 tbsp lemon juice

crème fraîche

ricotta cheese

powdered gelatine

lemon

strawberries

eggs

granulated sugar

1 Beat the ricotta cheese until smooth. Stir in the crème fraîche, sugar and lemon rind.

2 Place the lemon juice in a small bowl and sprinkle the gelatine over it. Place the bowl over a pan of hot water and stir to dissolve the gelatine completely.

3 Quickly stir the gelatine into the cheese mixture, mixing it in evenly.

4 Beat the egg whites until they form soft peaks. Quickly fold them into the cheese mixture.

5 Spoon the mixture into six lightly oiled, individual heart-shaped moulds and chill the moulds until set.

VARIATION

These little heart-shaped desserts are the perfect choice for a romantic dinner, but they don't have to be heart-shaped – try setting the mixture in individual fluted moulds, or even in ordinary teacups.

6 Place the strawberries and lemon juice in a blender and process until smooth. Place the turned-out hearts on serving plates and pour the sauce around them. Decorate with slices of strawberry.

Minted Raspberry Bavarois

A sophisticated dessert that can be made a day in advance for a special dinner party.

Serves 6

INGREDIENTS
450g/1lb/5½ cups raspberries
30ml/2 tbsp icing (confectioners')
   sugar
30ml/2 tbsp lemon juice
15ml/1 tbsp finely chopped
   fresh mint
30ml/2 tbsp/2 sachets powdered
   gelatine
75ml/5 tbsp boiling water
300ml/¼ pint/1¼ cups custard,
   made with skimmed milk
250g/9oz/1⅛ cups Greek
   (US strained plain) yogurt
fresh mint sprigs, to decorate

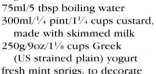

skimmed-milk custard

icing sugar

Greek yogurt

powdered gelatine

lemon

mint   *raspberries*

COOK'S TIP
You can make this dessert using frozen raspberries, which have a good colour and flavour. Allow them to thaw at room temperature, and use any juice in the jelly.

1 Reserve a few raspberries for decoration. Place the raspberries, icing sugar and lemon juice in a food processor and process until smooth.

2 Press the purée through a sieve (strainer) to remove the raspberry pips (seeds). Add the mint. You should have about 500ml/1 pint/2½ cups purée.

3 Sprinkle 5ml/1 tsp of the gelatine over 30ml/2 tbsp of the boiling water and stir until the gelatine has dissolved. Stir into 150ml/¼ pint/⅔ cup of the fruit purée.

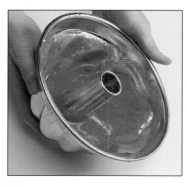

4 Pour this jelly into a 1-litre/1¾-pint/4-cup mould, and leave the mould to chill in the refrigerator until the jelly is just on the point of setting. Tip the mould to swirl the setting jelly around the sides, and then leave to chill until the jelly has set completely.

5 Stir the remaining fruit purée into the custard and yogurt. Dissolve the rest of the gelatine in the remaining water and stir it in quickly.

6 Pour the raspberry custard into the mould and leave it to chill until it has set completely. To serve, dip the mould quickly into hot water and then turn it out and decorate it with the reserved raspberries and the mint sprigs.

Cool Green Fruit Salad

A sophisticated, simple fruit salad for the summer.

Serves 6

INGREDIENTS
3 Ogen or Galia melons
115g/4oz green seedless grapes
2 kiwi fruit
1 star fruit (carambola)
1 green-skinned apple
1 lime
175ml/6fl oz/¾ cup sparkling
  grape juice

sparkling grape juice

melons

seedless grapes

kiwi fruit

star fruit

lime

green-skinned apple

COOK'S TIP

If you're serving this dessert on a hot summer day, serve the filled melon shells nestling on a platter of crushed ice to keep them beautifully cool.

1 Cut the melons in half and scoop out the seeds. Keeping the shells intact, scoop out the flesh with a melon baller, or scoop it out with a spoon and cut into bite-size cubes. Reserve the melon shells.

2 Remove any stems from the grapes, and, if they are large, cut them in half. Peel and chop the kiwi fruit. Thinly slice the star fruit. Core and thinly slice the apple and place the slices in a bowl with the melon, grapes, kiwi fruit and star fruit.

3 Thinly pare the rind from the lime and cut it in fine strips. Blanch the strips in boiling water for 30 seconds, and then drain them and rinse them in cold water. Squeeze the juice from the lime and toss it into the fruit.

4 Spoon the prepared fruit into the reserved melon shells and chill the shells in the refrigerator until required. Just before serving, spoon the sparkling grape juice over the fruit and sprinkle it with the lime rind.

Red Berry Sponge Tart

When soft berry fruits are in season, try making this delicious sponge tart. Serve warm from the oven with scoops of vanilla ice cream.

Serves 4

INGREDIENTS
softened butter, for greasing
450g/1lb/4 cups soft berry fruits
    such as raspberries, blackberries,
    blackcurrants, redcurrants,
    strawberries or blueberries
2 eggs, at room temperature
50g/2oz/¼ cup caster (superfine)
    sugar, plus extra, to
    taste (optional)
15ml/1 tbsp plain (all-purpose)
    flour
50g/2oz/¾ cup ground almonds
vanilla ice cream, to serve

eggs

ground almonds

flour
caster sugar
redcurrants
blackcurrants
raspberries
strawberries

1 Preheat the oven to 190°C/375°F/ Gas 5. Brush a 23cm/9in flan tin (tart pan) with softened butter and line the bottom with a circle of non-stick baking paper. Place the fruit in the bottom of the tin with a little sugar if they are tart.

2 Whisk the eggs and sugar together for about 3–4 minutes or until they leave a thick trail across the surface. Combine the flour and almonds, then fold into the egg mixture with a spatula – retaining as much air as possible.

3 Spread the mixture on top of the fruit base and bake in the preheated oven for 15 minutes. Turn out on to a serving plate and serve with vanilla ice cream.

VARIATION

When berry fruits are out of season, use bottled fruits, but ensure that they are well drained before use.

Strawberry Rose-petal Pashka

This lighter version of a traditional Russian dessert is ideal for dinner parties – make it a day or two in advance for best results.

Serves 4

INGREDIENTS
350g/12oz/1½ cups cottage cheese
175g/6oz/¾ cup low-fat natural
    (plain) yogurt
30ml/2 tbsp clear honey
2.5ml/½ tsp rose water
275g/10oz/2½ cups strawberries
handful of scented pink rose petals,
    to decorate

clear honey

cottage cheese   *rose water*

strawberries

natural yogurt

COOK'S TIP
The flowerpot shape is traditional for pashka, but you could make it in any shape – the small porcelain heart-shaped moulds with draining holes usually used for *coeurs à la crème* make a pretty alternative.

1 Drain any free liquid from the cottage cheese and tip the cheese into a sieve (strainer). Use a wooden spoon to rub it through the sieve into a bowl.

2 Stir the yogurt, honey and rose water into the cheese.

3 Roughly chop about half the strawberries and stir them into the cheese mixture.

4 Line a new, clean flowerpot or a sieve with fine muslin (cheesecloth) and tip the cheese mixture in. Leave it to drain over a bowl for several hours, or overnight.

5 Invert the flowerpot or sieve on to a serving plate, turn out the pashka and remove the muslin.

6 Decorate with the reserved strawberries and rose petals. Serve chilled.

Papaya Skewers with Passion Fruit Coulis

Tropical fruits, full of natural sweetness, make a simple, exotic dessert.

Serves 6

INGREDIENTS
3 ripe papayas
10 passion fruit or kiwi fruit
30ml/2 tbsp lime juice
30ml/2 tbsp icing (confectioners')
    sugar
30ml/2 tbsp white rum
toasted coconut, to garnish
    (optional)

papayas

icing sugar

passion fruit

lime

COOK'S TIP

If you are short of time, the passion fruit flesh can be used as it is, without puréeing or straining. Simply scoop it from the skins and mix it with the lime, sugar and rum. Kiwi fruit will still need to be puréed, however.

1 Cut the papayas in half and scoop out the seeds. Peel them and cut the flesh into even-size chunks. Thread the chunks on to six bamboo skewers.

2 Halve eight of the passion fruit or kiwi fruit and scoop out the flesh. Purée the flesh for a few seconds in a blender or food processor.

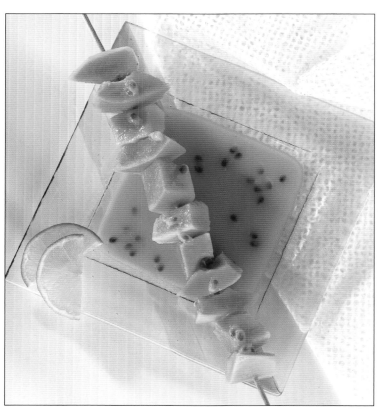

3 Press the pulp through a sieve (strainer) and discard the seeds. Add the lime juice, icing sugar and rum, and then stir well until the sugar has dissolved.

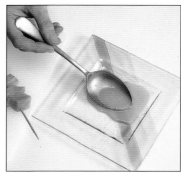

4 Spoon a little coulis on to six serving plates. Place the skewers on top. Scoop the flesh from the remaining passion fruit or kiwi fruit and spoon it over. Sprinkle with a little toasted coconut, if you like, and serve.

Figs with Ricotta Cream

Fresh, ripe figs are full of natural sweetness, and need little adornment. This simple recipe makes the most of their beautiful, intense flavour.

Serves 4

INGREDIENTS
4 ripe, fresh figs
115g/4oz/½ cup ricotta or
    cottage cheese
45ml/3 tbsp crème fraîche
15ml/1 tbsp clear honey
2.5ml/½ tsp vanilla extract
freshly grated nutmeg, to decorate

vanilla essence

clear honey

crème fraîche

ricotta cheese

figs

nutmeg

1 Trim the stalks from the figs. Make four cuts through each fig from the stalk end, cutting them almost through but leaving them joined at the base.

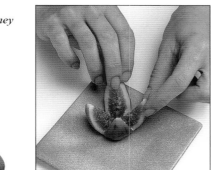

2 Place the figs on serving plates and open them out.

COOK'S TIP
If you prefer, the honey can be omitted and replaced with a little artificial sweetener.

3 Mix together the ricotta or cottage cheese, crème fraîche, honey and vanilla.

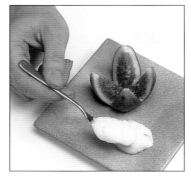

4 Spoon a little ricotta cream on to each plate and sprinkle with grated nutmeg to serve.

Fresh Citrus Jelly

Fresh fruit jellies really are worth the effort – they're packed with fresh flavour, natural colour and vitamins – and they make a lovely fat-free dessert.

Serves 4

INGREDIENTS
3 medium-size oranges
1 lemon
1 lime
300ml/½ pint/1¼ cups water
75g/3oz/⅓ cup golden caster (superfine) sugar
15ml/1 tbsp/1 sachet powdered gelatine
extra slices of fruit, to decorate

powdered gelatine

golden caster sugar

lime

oranges

lemon

1 With a sharp knife, cut all the peel and white pith from one orange and carefully remove the segments. Arrange the segments in the base of a 900ml/1½-pint/3¾-cup mould or dish.

2 Remove some shreds of citrus rind with a zester and reserve them for decoration. Grate the remaining rind from the lemon and lime and one orange. Place all the grated rind in a pan, with the water and sugar.

3 Heat gently, without boiling, until the sugar has dissolved. Remove from the heat. Squeeze the juice from all the rest of the fruit and stir it into the pan.

4 Strain the liquid into a measuring jug to remove the rind (you should have about 550ml/1 pint/2½ cups; if necessary, make up the amount with water). Sprinkle the gelatine over the liquid and stir until it has completely dissolved.

5 Pour a little of the jelly over the orange segments and chill until set. Leave the remaining jelly at room temperature to cool, but do not allow it to set.

COOK'S TIP

To speed up the setting of the fruit segments in jelly, stand the dish in a bowl of ice. Or, if you're short of time, simply stir the segments into the liquid jelly, pour into a serving dish and set it all together.

6 Pour the remaining cooled jelly into the dish and chill until set. To serve, turn out the jelly and decorate it with the reserved citrus rind shreds and slices of citrus fruit.

INDEX

INDEX